SHELTER
THEOLOGY

SHELTER THEOLOGY

———◇———

The Religious Lives of People without Homes

SUSAN J. DUNLAP

FORTRESS PRESS
Minneapolis

For Prasad and Anna

CONTENTS

PREFACE

Upon first sight of a person holding a sign at an intersection or a person wearing multiple layers of shaggy clothing on a hot day pushing a full shopping cart, the temptation is to look away. When hearing about the numbers of unhoused families with children, our reaction is often a numbness arising out of a sense of powerlessness to fix it. People living in extreme poverty seem so far away and "not like us" that we skip news reports about them.

Still, many people of faith who are moved by compassion and by vocation to address the social wound of poverty have focused on the urgent need for food, clothing, and housing through direct service or public advocacy. Far less frequently, we offer spiritual care. Even though poverty crushes the spirit as well as the body, and the life of faith confers much-needed dignity, perseverance, and hope, many who are engaged in ministry with people in extreme poverty avoid nurturing the life of faith.[1]

Haunting legacies of missionaries more interested in conversions than justice and urban missions that require Bible study before offering a meal may have clouded our judgment. Out of a desire to avoid mistakes of the past, we may have reduced the humanity of people living in poverty to a body in need and a life to be fixed while ignoring their often well-developed spiritual lives. This book records and honors the spiritual reasoning and resources

---

1. Laura Stivers states this in strong terms: "Satisfaction of spiritual needs is an entitlement of human personhood, as much for persons who are homeless as for persons who are housed." Stivers, *Disrupting Homelessness: Alternative Christian Approaches* (Minneapolis: Fortress, 2011), 8.

of people simply trying to survive life lived in material poverty, as well as attempting to emerge from its ravages. My desire is that this study will encourage the effort to minister to souls living in extreme poverty.

Our efforts to tend to the souls of people living without housing does not necessarily mean introducing something new; it does not mean bringing the correct version of the gospel or theologically sound content. It usually means nurturing the spiritual resources that people already hold. The pages that follow offer an insight into the religious worlds of people who live in extreme poverty, an insight that will deepen and enhance our capacity to respond to souls hungry for spiritual nurture in a difficult life.

Many of us have been forever changed by liberation theology's proclamation of "God's preferential option for the poor." This includes "epistemological privilege," a priority granted to the theological judgments of people living in the deprivations of poverty.[2] Yet there has been scant research into the actual content and practices of the faith of America's poor. If some of us are seeking to honor God's preferential option for the poor and to grant epistemological privilege not only regarding social, economic, and political power dynamics but also theological insight, then it is necessary to study what actual people living under the strain of poverty concretely believe and practice.

A study of the theology of people living in extreme poverty reveals facility in doing theology. Theological nuance, skilled application of a fitting Scripture verse to a troubling situation, and empathic reading of others' hunger for God are just some of the capacities they displayed. While in many cases, educational levels are low and formal theological education is absent, there is nevertheless intellectual and pastoral reasoning that responds nimbly, strategically, and compassionately to a variety of trying circumstances.

As many mainline white congregations face liturgical, spiritual, and intellectual calcification in the face of rising tides of social, economic, and political complexity and threat, here are novel voices that are practiced in surviving in trying circumstances. Many of us are moved by a desire to go beyond comfortable religious worlds,

2. Kenneth Himes et al., eds., *Modern Catholic Social Teaching* (Washington, DC: Georgetown University Press, 2005), 323.

beyond places that confirm what we already know, into relationships with people who struggle with the challenges of living in extreme poverty. This book offers that invitation and points the way to relationships of mutual respect, vulnerability, and challenge.

How I Got Here

Ten years ago, as a teacher of the art of pastoral care, I realized the importance of also being a practitioner of that art. Efforts at finding work in hospital chaplaincy and congregational ministry did not pan out. As a practitioner, I was professionally homeless. Eventually, the insight emerged that I could go "into the streets and lanes of the town and bring in the poor, the crippled, the blind, and the lame" (Luke 14:21). So I walked into the office of the director of Urban Ministries of Durham (UMD) and said, "I would like to be the shelter chaplain, and you don't have to pay me."

The director immediately accepted my offer, and I began working there three mornings per week. As UMD has done for thousands of others, a space was made for me. UMD provides emergency shelter and three meals a day every day of the year. The people I serve are staying in the shelter and homeless, or they are nearby residents who take meals at UMD. Durham, North Carolina, has several well-established, secluded camps inhabited by people without permanent housing who panhandle at street corners, but the people I see are usually not from this population. My "congregation" is from the lowest socioeconomic stratum of Durham. Some live in shotgun shacks built in the 1920s. Others live in large public housing complexes. Still others have no place to live and survive by "couch hopping" among friends and families' homes, and some sleep on church steps, in urban shrubbery, under a freeway overpass, in patches of woods scattered by the railroad tracks, in parking garages, in cars, in abandoned houses.

Around UMD, there are "worlds," social worlds with history, characters, monikers, habits, inside jokes, mutual give-and-take, roles, and mores. If not centered on the UMD site, they clearly include the UMD-linked space. For example, among the people gathered along the parking lot bordered by a high fence, there are clusters of worlds. There is a Hispanic world; the old-timer world; and the younger, hip world, for example. These are not ideal worlds. They include betrayal, violence, and exploitation. But they are worlds, and they confer friendship and a degree of belonging and identity.

As a chaplain, I nurture an additional world, that of the Prayer Service. We meet three mornings a week to offer each other prayers, testimony, and music, as well as support and ongoing community. There are no sermons, no orders of worship, no songbooks. Rather, the content is provided by whoever is in attendance that day. The Prayer Service world is imperfect, fragile, and brief, but nevertheless, for some people some of the time, it is a zone of dignity, hope, shared compassion, agency, creativity, and peace. It spills out into relationships with people beyond the Prayer Service as well. Through the Prayer Service, I have met people who bring life, color, and kindness into a very difficult world.

In the course of these years as a chaplain, I became drawn to the often-repeated *forms* and *content* of the spiritual resources they brought.[3] There is an archive, a cache, of theological beliefs and practices that many people have called upon to find hope, to understand their circumstances, to find the stamina to keep on living, to create alternative worlds. Eventually, I began writing down my descriptions of events and stories that I witnessed. After receiving approval from my university's Institutional Review Board (IRB), I began a more formal study that included over forty interviews, mostly at UMD but also at other agencies that offer services to

---

3. At times the chaplain and the researcher have conflicting aims. The researcher encourages the other to speak with minimal interference, commentary, or interpretation of their words. However, as a *clergy* researcher, I refuse to bracket my chaplain identity during an interview, which means protecting and even ministering to the interviewee prevail over any research aim. Therefore, I am judicious about pushing for details in areas that might retraumatize the interviewee. I may ask one or two follow-up questions, but I will respect the boundary they have established. If my pastoral instincts suggest that an empathic response is called for, I will offer one immediately. I will also offer community resources, a counternarrative, a biblical text, or prayer if pastoral concerns lead me there. This mixed motivation, and the priority I give to my role as chaplain, will all be considered in the analysis of the interviews. The imperative for all qualitative researchers is to name our positioning to self and reader and offer a reading of the data with this positionality in clear view.

people in poverty.[4] Though I received permission to publish the words from each person I interviewed, here and there I have changed details of identifying characteristics, such as appearance, history, and life events, in order to protect their privacy. My hope is that I will remain faithful to their inner and outer religious worlds and thus communicate the humanity, dignity, and complexity of people living on the margins and recognize their lives, loves, losses, insights, struggles, and accomplishments. This study is not meant to be representative of all people who live without homes, nor is it meant to be representative of everyone who frequents UMD. It is primarily based on a subset of people who have identified themselves as people of faith.

I will fall short of accurately rendering the particularities and richness and sustaining power of the religious lives of the people I studied. I will get it wrong. I will distort it. I will magnify the insignificant and miss the significant.[5] More malignant is that I will mischaracterize people in a demeaning, infantilizing, or blaming way or that I will reproduce offensive stereotypes of people living in poverty. Dwelling in a toxic cultural soup that holds negative views of the people living in poverty renders any researcher vulnerable to absorbing and reproducing them. With all white Americans, I have been steeped in the sin of white supremacy, and my perceptions and interpretations will no doubt reflect that. Standing in the Calvinist tradition, fully convinced that sin infects everything human beings are and do, I confess my eyes are shaped by racist spectacles, my ears hear through classist filters, and assessments I make are no doubt guided by assumptions of superiority based on academic credentials. I also fear I will romanticize "the poor" or make a spectacle of their suffering or that I have a bit of the voyeur within me who wants to watch pain from the safety of whiteness and economic privilege

---

4. Research institutions are required to have IRBs in order to ensure the ethical treatment of human subjects of research.

5. One researcher studying aboriginal people in Australia spoke of the errors in earlier researchers' perceptions: "The Whites saw nothing in the fringe camps except deprivation and disorder. They were unaware of the meanings, pleasures and desires within this disordered cultural sphere, or of the community's history and memories." Gillian Cowlishaw, "Race at Work: Reflecting on Fieldwork in the Northern Territory," *Journal of the Royal Anthropological Institute* 3, no. 4 (1997): 96.

without costly personal investment for the sake of change.[6] There are many risks of sin, distortion, and failure in this project.

One example of how the dynamics of race and gender can distort my research became clear in a casual conversation with a Black man who was a client of UMD. I was describing my participation in a public conversation on race, and I started by saying, "As a white woman . . ." He interrupted me and said simply, "You're not a white woman." When I asked what he meant, he replied, "White women are scared of Black men. You're not scared." My eyes were opened to the possibility that some men at UMD approach me with the assumption that I feel threatened, and thus I am a danger to them. This no doubt rendered them on guard, cautious about any behavior that might cause me to summon the authorities of UMD staff or even law enforcement. Another time, Missionary Richey, a leader of the Prayer Service, was talking with a Black man and my name came up. He said, "She's not white; she's nice." When I pressed her on what he meant, she said he probably thought being a white person meant I was "mean." Again, I expected people to think I would not understand or I would be clueless, controlling, or condescending. I did not expect people to think I would be mean. I learned that my white female body exuded danger, especially to Black men, and I wondered about the many times my whiteness had evoked caution. There are far more men than women at UMD, and most of my interviews were with Black men. The assumption that I was "scared" or "mean" undoubtedly affected the quality of my research.

These fears of sin, distortion, and failure held me back, and I resisted writing this book for several years. It was when talking to a wise friend that I recognized a final, very powerful fear: not being able to do justice to the moments of sacred connection in our Prayer Service community, not being able to honor the holiness of some of the stories I have heard, not being able to fully express the Godness of the stories, prayers, transformations, redemptions, and

---

6. The term *poorism* has been coined to describe tourist incursions into the slums of Rio de Janeiro, Mumbai, Nairobi, and other large cities in order to view impoverished communities. Some claim it is voyeuristic, intrusive, and exploitive; others believe it is a means of consciousness raising for privileged travelers. One tourist was "staying at a posh Taj Hotel in Mumbai where, he noted, a bottle of Champagne cost the equivalent of two years' salary for many Indians." Eric Weiner, "Slum Visits: Tourism or Voyeurism?," *New York Times*, March 9, 2008, https://tinyurl.com/y3eb4ty6.

encounters that I have witnessed in my work as a chaplain. My wise friend, who has also written about great suffering and deep faith, quickly reminded me that all our attempts to write about what we have seen and heard are akin to writing about nothing less than the numinous, inexpressible, unfathomable God whom we worship. Her words reassured me. Of course, I won't get it all right, because of my sinful eyes and ears, yes, but also because of the presence of a God whose redeeming love is beyond human ken and pen.

CROSSCONTEXT FRUITS AND RISKS

So I proceed, recognizing that the vast majority of people I have worked with and interviewed are Black, and it might be the height of presumptuousness for me to make comments, even positive assessments, about the beliefs and practices that have emerged out of the Black Church. There are legitimate questions about my authority to speak of the content and function of beliefs from a social, religious, cultural context removed from my own. It could easily be said that my ignorance; the power dynamics; the lack of shared experience of my tradition, family, and self with the Black Church; and the blinders of white privilege completely delegitimize my discussion of these matters.[7] So with humility and with hope, I offer these reasons for why I make these comments anyway.

There are others like me—white, seminary-educated, mainstream Protestants—who work as chaplains in institutions where there are people from backgrounds similar to the people at UMD. Black readers will likely be familiar with what I describe in these pages; my conversations with Black scholars have confirmed this assumption. However, this material may be new to chaplains from my demographic who are working in prisons, hospitals, hospice, nursing homes, and the military among people who hold to the beliefs and practices I have described, and I hope to contribute to their skills in pastoral caregiving. I hope to lay the groundwork for

---

7. In fact, it was a Presbyterian, James Thornwell, who was a prime architect of the theological justification of slavery. Why should someone from his tradition be trusted with speaking about the religious beliefs and practices of descendants of enslaved people, whose enslavement he justified?

a respectful appreciation for these beliefs and practices and provide a deeper understanding of how they function to mediate God's salvific action, how they sustain and provide links to a community of people, how they are forms of resistance. I hope to model a humility, openness, empathy, and respect for belief systems different from mine. Writing about my encounters, including what was surprising or jarring, may inform others like me working with a similar population.

The potential for exploitation of people living in poverty through mishandled representations is offset to a degree if the researcher is actively involved in advocacy work that addresses that poverty. My church is a member of Durham CAN (congregations, associations, and neighborhoods), a form of community organizing connected with the Industrial Areas Foundation founded by Saul Alinsky. I have been particularly involved in advocating for the construction of affordable housing on two nearby parking lots, one immediately between UMD and my church. We leaders in Durham CAN met with the county manager; with individual county commissioners, builders, developers; and with other advocacy organizations. We met with the organization that facilitates public-private partnerships. We asked an architect to sketch out how many housing units might be possible. We spoke at the board of county commissioners' public meetings. We went to all of the community listening sessions. At our Delegates Assembly where we brought together over five hundred people from our member organizations, we witnessed the commissioners' public commitment to affordable housing on those lots. The fact of my engagement in addressing injustices faced by the people I am studying further authorizes this study.

I also write in order to surface the theological perspectives and religious habits of people who live without homes or in extreme poverty, to recognize them as practical theological thinkers. I seek to honor the theological facility of people rarely recognized beyond being someone who needs to be fixed, helped, pitied, or changed. There is risk in not writing this book. It is the risk of participating in the forces that render invisible and insignificant the people whom I work with. Nancy Scheper-Hughes says, "Seeing, listening, touching, recording, can be, if done with care and sensitivity, acts of fraternity and sisterhood, acts of solidarity. Above all they are the work of recognition. *Not to look, not to touch, not to record, can be the hostile act, the act of indifference and of turning away."*[8] Trusting that not to look—and not to speak—is a form of hostility, even an act of violence, I risk embarking on this journey of attempting to represent while being changed by the people I serve at the shelter.

So I proceed, trusting in the power of God to redeem all our feeble and sinful efforts. My hope is that it will serve some good, that I will help some people feel that their suffering has borne fruit for the sake of others, and that I have been faithful to people who have entrusted me with their stories, testimonies, and prayers.

Because language can both create and obscure, disclose and distort, I want to say a word about the language I use to refer to the people I know and work with from UMD. I usually use "person-first" language. Rather than saying "homeless people," or "the homeless," or "poor people," I have said "people living without homes" or "people living in extreme poverty." The US Interagency Council on Homelessness refers to "people experiencing homelessness." Similarly, rather than saying "the mentally ill," I have spoken of "people living with mental illness." Rather than referring to "addicts" or "alcoholics," I have written "people living with a substance use disorder." However, when speaking theologically, I have usually referred to "the poor" in order to maintain a linguistic connection to Scripture, in particular to maintain the resonance with Jesus's use of the word *poor*. When describing his ministry to John the Baptist, he says, "The poor have good news brought to them" (Matt 11:5), and his image of the Great Feast includes "the poor, the crippled, the lame, and the blind" (Luke 14:13). He tells the crowd in the Sermon on the Plain, "Blessed are you who are poor" (Luke 6:20). Also, I want to maintain a theological connection to the thread of liberation theology's language of the preferential option for the poor. "The poor" carries rich theological and biblical meaning that I want to preserve.

---

8. Nancy Scheper-Hughes, *Death without Weeping: The Violence of Everyday Life in Brazil* (Berkeley: University of California Press, 1992), 28, quoted in Mark Lewis Taylor, "Subalternity and Advocacy as Kairos for Theology," in *Opting for the Margins: Postmodernity and Liberation in Christian Theology*, ed. Joerg Rieger (New York: Oxford University Press, 2003), 38 (emphasis mine).

ACKNOWLEDGMENTS

I want to thank the three directors of Urban Ministries of Durham (UMD) with whom I have worked. Lloyd Schmiedler first welcomed me, Patrice Nelson offered practical and spiritual support, and Sheldon Mitchell has given me the space to continue serving as chaplain.

Valerie Cooper sparked the idea that the theology I was hearing at the Prayer Service is a form of resistance. Mark Chaves, Cynthia Curtis, Wib Gulley, Connel Fullencamp, and Terry Allebaugh offered helpful conversation.

I especially want to thank the readers who read all or part of the manuscript: Kim Abels, Travis Albritton, Chuck Campbell, Kelli Dugan, Mary McClintock Fulkerson, Sarah Jobe, John P. Lee, Jerusha Neal, Denise Thorpe, and Jane Williams.

Many thanks to David Lorimer, who provided copyediting. Great gratitude goes to Carey Newman for his patience during long, really long, fallow periods, for reading draft upon draft, and for many meetings and phone calls. His encouragement and belief in this project sustained me.

During times when this ministry was painful, I am grateful for the people who helped me through. Support for my ministry has also been support for this book about it, so I thank Susan Hazlett, Patrice Nelson, Karen Stewart, and the Women's Spiritual Formation class, in particular Kathy Conner, Catherine Dumas, and Sharon Hirsch, whose work on the margins continues to inspire me.

Kate Joyce and Mary McClintock Fulkerson offered friendship, insight, and lots of assurance that this was a worthwhile project. Mary's work as my teacher and as a writer provided the foundation and inspiration for this book, just as she has paved the way for so many other scholars.

I also want to acknowledge the people I met at the shelter who died untimely deaths: Carla, Coco, Darlene, Danny, Eric, Julius, Lee, Linda, Mike, Mimi, Wallace, Shonda, Tasmania, and the Artist.

My deep gratitude goes to the people who passed through the Prayer Service and shared encouragement, struggles, songs, Scripture. I thank the people I interviewed, who trusted me enough to go to painful places as they told their stories, especially the people whose stories I told at length. In recent years, George, Josh, and Joe, along with John and Nancy, have been especially present. John P. Lee offered steadfast leadership, friendship, singing, record keeping, articles, and prayers. Nancy Ross brought singing, words of encouragement, friendship, prayers, Scripture, and sayings.

Lilac and Patch spoke no words, but their steadfast presence helped this book get written. My parents—Jean, who has gone before us, and Harold—and my brothers, Paul and Kent, ground me in my deepest sense of who I am and what I am called to do. Anna transcribed interviews and brought me coffee, pies, and Elmo, and she delights my soul beyond measure. Finally, I thank Prasad, with whom I share the deepest laughter and life. He is unsurpassed in the giving of himself to the people he loves.

CHAPTER I

WOUNDS OF POVERTY

Leaving the homeless shelter at night, I see a remarkable sight that captures a truth about my home. Ahead of me on the right is the sparkling new Durham Performing Arts Center, built in 2008. The entire front wall is glass, and when a performance is beginning or ending, I see people walking back and forth on three levels, going up and down on the staircases diagonally between these levels. Into the dark night, there is a blaze of light that discloses not only living people but also large posters of artistic performances of the past and present. The transparent glass walls reveal the presence of bodies in motion even as the art posters speak of performances that reveal truths of life and love, good and evil, the tragedies and triumphs of the world.

On the left side of the street rises another wall, taller and wider, made up of large expanses of unperforated white cement. Interrupting this expanse are horizontal rows of slits, from which no light escapes, and larger rows of outdoor hallways encased in fencing, lit by greenish-yellowish light. No human bodies are visible, and the building bears no adornment. This building is the county jail. One of these edifices is open and disclosing; the other is sealed and enclosing. When built in 2003, the jail was the largest capital investment the Durham, North Carolina, community had ever made.

The performing arts center represents the start of downtown Durham's rebirth. We have always had a developed counterculture, with multiple nonprofit social justice organizations and a corpus of people who are devoted to the Durham Bulls and our colorful Ninth Street shopping area. In the last couple of decades, our edginess has expanded as the arts flourished, and our IT and biotech firms have multiplied. Now Durham is growing rapidly, with thousands of high-end residences newly built downtown and trendy restaurants and boutiques moving in. Originally defined by tobacco, Durham is now a center of creative, cultural, and scientific developments.

On the other side of the street, the jail represents the part of Durham that our city and nation have failed. The criminal justice system and poverty interact in complicated ways.[1] As I work with people who are living without shelter, I learn that the jail is the largest deliverer of mental health care, it may be the only place of refuge during the coldest months, and it houses a disproportionate number of impoverished people who cannot afford court fines and fees, as well as people I know who have committed minor crimes trying to survive. This other Durham consistently deals with higher poverty rates than the average rate of poverty in North Carolina. The percent of Durham residents living below the poverty line is 17.1, and 7.8 percent live in deep poverty, with incomes less than $13,000 for a family of four.[2] Poverty is mapped onto race in Durham: there are very roughly equal numbers of Blacks and whites in Durham, yet there are three times as many Blacks living in poverty as there are white people living in poverty. We live in an economically, culturally, and racially divided city.

DURHAM, NORTH CAROLINA

Like in many cities in America, it is possible to arrange one's life in complete oblivion to poverty in one's community. This oblivion

---

1. For an excellent explication of this interaction, see Peter Edelman, *Not a Crime to Be Poor: The Criminalization of Poverty in America* (New York: New Press, 2017); and Karen Dolan and Jody Carr, "The Poor Get Prison: The Alarming Spread of the Criminalization of Poverty," Institute for Policy Studies, March 18, 2015, https://tinyurl.com/y8jrr4fn.
2. "Durham, North Carolina (NC) Poverty Rate Data—Information about Poor and Low Income Residents," City-Data, accessed August 9, 2019, https://tinyurl.com/y3sgaevu.

is not necessarily because of geographic distance. For example, I worship at a downtown church, one-half block from Urban Ministries of Durham (UMD), the homeless shelter and community café, which offers "food, shelter, and a future to neighbors in need." Yet there is an invisible line at my church's border that most members of my church rarely cross. I go just over that line when I go to UMD, but it was only recently that I went farther past that line on foot. A man from the addiction recovery program invited me and my friend and cochaplain Missionary Richey to walk deeper into the area past UMD. As we walked along a main street, lined with small homes and public housing, he began to point out landmarks. Gesturing into the cluster of buildings in the public housing development, he pointed to a large pile of rocks, saying, "Lots of drug deals there. You can hide when the police show up." On the other side of the street, he pointed out the small house where Latino men go to pay for sex and then to the one where Black men go for the same purpose. As we walked, I pointed to a house and asked a question. Our guide quickly told me to stop pointing because it put us in danger, for reasons I did not understand. He was quite adamant about it, as I found out because I kept forgetting his warning.

When we came to the railroad tracks, he pointed out a mattress in the distance, in the weeds under a railroad bridge, where the common mixture of crack use and sex is found. As we continued our walk, our guide showed us the house where white men go to find sex workers, and at that moment, two white women came out, chatting, smiling. Our guide told us that they were a mother and daughter who worked there. I was shaken by the realization that this world is merely blocks from the church where my daughter was baptized, where we go every week for worship, where she leaves for church camp, where our renovated sanctuary hosts the Ciompi Quartet from Duke University, where our pipe organ plays Bach, Beethoven, Widor, and Rutter. In other urban settings, such as Washington, DC, or New York, such juxtapositions of plenitude and poverty are perhaps more visible. But it is rarer in our small city, and the proximity of the two worlds was a jarring reminder of the gross inequalities that characterize Durham.

It would be false to claim that there are literally two self-contained, homogeneous Durhams that can be distinguished and described accurately. It would diminish the complexity of both, elide the overlapping networks, and hide generations of exploitive relations between the two. It would also erase the sizable Latino population in Durham. Yet speaking of two Durhams highlights the fact of both inequality and separate spheres of daily living. My family and I live, work, shop, and worship in one part of Durham, and three mornings a week, I work in a very different Durham at UMD.

In this other Durham, people also live, work, shop, and worship, yet many of us live as if this other one did not exist. I am particularly interested in describing the lives of people living in extreme poverty, which is half the poverty rate. In the United States, forty million people live in poverty, which is an annual income of roughly $26,000 for a family of four. However, the population I will focus on lives in extreme poverty, which is $13,000 or less per year for a family of four, or about $6,000 for an individual.[3] Even more specifically, I wish to lift up the religious lives of people living under these circumstances of extreme poverty. People engage in religious practices and make religious utterances in a particular context. In order to understand the meaning and function of the religious language and practices of the people in the shelter, it is necessary to surface the context in which it emerges.

As I drive by, each building holds hundreds of people. I assume the gap between them has never been crossed—people in the jail have never attended the performing arts center, and people enjoying an evening at the theater have never been inside the jail. These two worlds rarely meet in Durham, and this scene vividly illustrates that.

POVERTY IN DURHAM

When I first started working at the shelter, I would look at the groups of people congregated outside, or at the roughly two hundred people eating in the café, and I would wonder, *How did this happen?* How did it happen that in a portion of our city, there are people who simply have nothing to eat and no place to sleep? The group of men who gathered just across the street, sitting at the base of a parking

---

3. Center for Poverty Research, "What Is 'Deep Poverty'?," University of California at Davis, accessed February 9, 2018, https://poverty.ucdavis.edu/faq/what-deep -poverty.

lot fence, day after day, how did they end up there? *How does a town evolve to the place where this is how a portion of its population lives?*

Durham is not a typical southern city. It did not endure the Civil War as did Atlanta, Richmond, and New Orleans. Rather, at the end of the Civil War, we were just a railroad stop among scattered buildings and farms between Raleigh and Hillsborough. But our brightleaf tobacco proved to be very popular with Union troops who stopped here for the large-scale surrender of Confederate troops at Bennett Place, and when they got back home up North, they wanted more. That is how Durham became the home of Bull Durham tobacco and the Duke family's American Tobacco.

Around the same time, newly emancipated Blacks came from rural areas to Durham looking for jobs. Within a few decades, people formerly enslaved and their children and grandchildren were able to build a thriving, culturally rich, and socially interconnected area known as Hayti. The location of the area was defined by strict laws of segregation, which meant Blacks had only one place to spend their money, and so they spent it in the Black-owned stores, movie theater, hotels, barbers, and so on. The more prosperous citizens of Hayti—the Moores, Merricks, and Spaldings—built neoclassical mansions along Fayetteville Street. The educational precursors of North Carolina Central University provided an educational and cultural center, and close-knit social groups flourished. Not only did W. E. B. Du Bois visit Durham in the early twentieth century, but he wrote a favorable article for the monthly publication the *World's Work* called "The Upbuilding of Black Durham: The Success of the Negroes and Their Value to a Tolerant and Helpful Southern City."[4] About Durham, he said,

> To-day there is a singular group in Durham where a black man may get up in the morning from a mattress made by black men, in a house which a black man built out of lumber which black men cut and planed; he may put on a suit which he bought at a colored haberdashery and socks knit at a colored mill; he may cook victuals from a colored grocery

---

4. W. E. B. Du Bois, "The Upbuilding of Black Durham: The Success of the Negroes and Their Value to a Tolerant and Helpful Southern City," *World's Work* 23 (January 1912): 334–38.

on a stove which black men fashioned; he may earn his living working for colored men, be sick in a colored hospital,
and buried from a colored church; and the Negro insurance
society will pay his widow enough to keep his children in a
colored school. This is surely progress.[5]

Durham's Hayti was on the national map for being a thriving, prosperous, culturally developed community.

From Hayti and other parts of Durham, Blacks worked jobs in
textiles and tobacco, which provided most of the lower-wage pay-
roll. My friend and cochaplain tells me about going to the tobacco
factory where her grandmother came out with a scarf on her head,
smelling like tobacco, and every Thursday she got a Popsicle. The
jobs were menial, but they provided a steady wage. One former
tobacco worker, Mr. Horace Higgins, said, "From 1945 on, Liggett
and Myers paid good wages, and American (too). . . . You could
get a good living. . . . Colored folks got good jobs, got to be foremen." In those early years, the work was hot, dirty, smelly, loud, and
sometimes dangerous. Mrs. Roxie McCullough said, "Back then,
the foremen, they were all white [and] we were all black. The white
people were in another part (in the factory). Stemming was dirty,
dusty, sweaty and it paid way down lower than what whites got."
Mr. William Preston (Pratt) Edwards said, "They'd give the white
man six cents and the black man three cents. . . . I was angry all the
time."[6] The jobs were neither just nor easy, but tobacco jobs formed
the backbone of the economy and of Black wages.

However, there were strong forces inhibiting Hayti's further
economic development. Like many cities in America, redlining
consigned to decay parts of the city occupied by Blacks.[7] One of the
redlining maps in Durham marked an area considered less valuable

---

5. Du Bois, 338.
6. Beverly Jones, Claudia Egelhoff, and Roger Manley, *Working in Tobacco: An Oral
History of Durham's Tobacco Factory Workers* (Durham, NC: History Department,
North Carolina Central University, 1987), 22, 25, 30.
7. *Redlining* refers to maps used by the federal government to systematically exclude
Blacks from receiving loans to buy or maintain homes. And in America, homeown-
ership has been the way for families to accrue wealth. These maps outlined in red
the areas considered the least desirable for offering bank loans, and these areas were
overwhelmingly occupied by people of color.

with the assessment "This was formerly a good white residential street, but negroes are gradually taking up the area."[8] I currently live in an area that was given an *A* designation on the map created in the 1930s, which meant it was the most attractive to loan makers. Notes on the map about my neighborhood recorded "favorable influences," which included a "public park, *restricted covenants and deeds*, adequate utilities."[9] Seeking specifics about these covenants and deeds, I went to the city's office of the Register of Deeds and found a 1923 deed for our property with the following text: "No property or building shall be owned or occupied by the colored race."[10] Only one-half mile from my house is an area given a *D* designation with the label "*infiltration* of Negro population slowly increasing."[11] Buttressed by reports funded by the federal government, Hayti was systematically barred from access to many financial resources, and the racist economic legacy persists.

Though Hayti's development was crimped by such policies as redlining, most devastating was a freeway built in the sixties that sliced through the middle of it, destroying structures, homes, businesses, social spaces, and cultural history. Business slowed down, social networks were weakened, cultural offerings decreased, and the population declined.

With gains made during the civil rights era, formerly white-owned and -frequented businesses were desegregated, and it became possible for Blacks to spend their money outside Hayti, and businesses further suffered.[12] Redlining, desegregation, and the Durham Freeway have not served the economic well-being of Hayti well.

In the 1980s, the textile mills and tobacco factories began to shut down, following national trends. The disappearance of these sorts of jobs around the country has been called the largest

8. Area description of Durham, NC, Tim Maps, accessed August 9, 2020, https://tinyurl.com/y5d8dyhb.

9. Bull City 150, "Uneven Ground," Home Owners Loan Corporation Map, 1939, https://tinyurl.com/y2uwknst (emphasis mine).

10. Registered in Durham County Register of Deeds, book 66, July 2, 1923, 417.

11. Durham Country Register of Deeds (emphasis mine). Also excluded were swine and other livestock. People of the "colored race" were allowed to live on our property if the owner built a separate building for the servants.

12. See Osha Gray Davis, *Best of Enemies: Race and Redemption in the New South* (Chapel Hill: University of North Carolina Press, 2007), for a compelling account of efforts for civil rights in Durham.

7

cause of the rise in poverty rates in the last few decades.[13] The departure of low-skilled, often difficult, low-paying but nevertheless stable jobs gutted the lives of the people living in poverty in Durham. By 1986, the last of the Erwin Cotton Mills shut down. In 1987, American Tobacco had left Durham, and Liggett and Myers closed its Durham plant in 1999. New jobs were largely in the biotech area, not suitable for people with high school or less education or in unstable minimum-wage service jobs. The low-skill jobs that had been steady for years had moved out. Durham in the eighties and nineties was not an economically vibrant place. Downtown had little vitality, there were empty buildings here and there, and it was virtually empty after sundown.

In 1995, a new Durham Bulls Athletic Park was built downtown, replacing the classic old ballpark featured in the movie *Bull Durham*. Ten years later, next door, the renovated, enormous American Tobacco campus opened with office space, restaurants, an outdoor concert stage, a YMCA, and a place for people downtown to rejuvenate in the grassy lawn bordered by an artificial stream. Within four years, the regionally successful Durham Performing Arts Center opened, hosting such stars as Willie Nelson, Jamie Foxx, Jerry Seinfeld, and Diana Ross. Broadway musicals from *The Sound of Music* to *Hamilton* performed on its stage. About three thousand new high-end residential units were constructed within about five years, up from practically no downtown residences.[14] Durham has been written up in the *New York Times* as a foodie town with innovative cuisine and an emphasis on buying local.[15] *Bon Appétit, Southern Living*, and the *New York Post* have all written about Durham's food scene.

At the same time, an ongoing affordable housing crisis plagues Durham.[16] Property near downtown Durham is rapidly being gentrified, forcing many low-income renters to move out of old

---

13. Michael B. Katz, *The Undeserving Poor: America's Enduring Confrontation with Poverty* (Oxford: Oxford University Press, 2013), 161.

14. "State of Downtown Durham 2018," Downtown Durham, Inc., accessed October 26, 2018, https://tinyurl.com/y2ffyjsk.

15. Ingrid Williams, "Durham Dining: Pies, Panini and Barbecue," *New York Times*, June 24, 2011, https://tinyurl.com/yy7wwcmq.

16. Dawn Vaughn Baumgardner, "Durham in an 'Affordable Housing Crisis,' Council Members Say," *Durham Herald-Sun*, March 21, 2018, https://tinyurl.com/y2hwcl3d.

neighborhoods to housing toward the edge of Durham. They are uprooted from place, community, and routine; are often farther from church, employment, and social services; and end up with limited access to public transportation. From time to time over the last ten years, I have driven with Missionary Richey through her childhood neighborhood near downtown, and she points out where she used to live with her grandmother, where her sister had a funeral for a cat, and where they used to put lightning bugs on their ears for earrings. The small, older, wooden homes with front porches and shady sidewalks serve as touchstones for many stories that illustrate life several decades ago in this area that has remained home for Black families.[17] Now, as we drive through this neighborhood, many of the homes are newly painted a trendy color, a hybrid car is parked in the driveway, an expensive bike sits on the porch, and a sign for a progressive cause is stuck in the lawn. One neighborhood woman said that when the police start patrolling the neighborhood, you can tell white people are moving in. Our drives through this gentrifying neighborhood have illustrated changes in housing patterns that are to the detriment of people who need housing that is affordable.

Durham is not the only city with an affordable housing crisis. What is noteworthy is that "this crisis of housing insecurity is erupting in America's richest, most rapidly developing cities."[18] As people and businesses move in, property values go up, and housing becomes less affordable. And furthermore, "unlike earlier periods of widespread homelessness and displacement, such as during the recession of 2008, what we're witnessing today is an emergency born less of poverty than prosperity—*occurring not despite but precisely because of the economic boom*."[19] Durham is growing economically, and many are benefitting from the arts, entertainment, jobs, and sense of vibrancy and well-being that accompanies such

---

17. Mel Norton, researcher and activist, spoke of the "high levels of disinvestment" that specific neighborhoods experienced. Norton says, "They didn't become disinvested overnight. This is direct result of racially discriminatory policies on the federal, state and local level." Lisa Sorg, "Take 5: Durham's Gentrification Challenge," *News and Observer*, November 3, 2015, https://tinyurl.com/y2vf62vd.

18. Brian Goldstone, "The New American Homeless," *New Republic*, August 21, 2019, https://tinyurl.com/yy446hpc.

19. Goldstone (emphasis mine).

growth. However, there is a cost to the enjoyment of the latest nou-
veau cuisine at yet another restaurant opening downtown. Precisely
because of this economic growth, many in Durham are experiencing displacement from familiar neighborhoods and institutions, the
stress and shame of eviction, and even homelessness.

There are, of course, many more contributions to the evolution
of poverty in Durham. We could also speak of racism in the history of public education, incarceration patterns, and availability of
groceries, for example. Furthermore, it is not completely accurate
to say that the history of Black Durham is the history of poverty in
Durham. This brief account is only a beginning to a rough understanding of how my city came to be the way it is and why, when
I look out at the fence outside UMD, when I look over the café,
there are people gathered without shelter, income, or meaningful
networks of care, and the vast majority are Black.

GLOBAL TRENDS AND LOCAL EFFECTS

It is not only local forces that have contributed to the shape of
poverty in Durham. The loss of stable, low-wage jobs can be
understood as part of larger economic forces under the canopy of
neoliberalism, dubbed "capitalism on steroids." While the intellectual origins of neoliberalism began decades earlier, neoliberal
economic policy took root in the 1980s under the leadership of
Prime Minister Margaret Thatcher in England and President Ronald Reagan in the United States. Under classical capitalism, the
world of finance and business is to be left free of governmental restraint. However, neoliberal economic policies are usually
accompanied by government policies that not only refrain from
regulating corporations but act as the servant of corporate interests. Neoliberal capitalism has been accompanied by public policy
in active service of corporate business interests, such as crimp-
ing the power of unions, lowering taxes on corporations, gutting
safety and environmental regulations, cutting funds for social services, and privatizing such public institutions as jails and schools.
Durham's loss of jobs to overseas sites is part of the effects of neoliberal modes of thinking and acting.

One pastoral theologian explored the impact of the emergence of neoliberal capitalism on souls and communities.[20] Over the three decades of his pastoral counseling practice, he noticed a change among clients' accounts of their lives. Not only did they face issues of mental health, family crisis, unemployment, or a troubled past, but they were more and more likely to blame themselves for these problems. He eventually placed the blame on the hyperindividualism of our neoliberal age—who or what else can be blamed if it is believed that individuals have the freedom and power to make of their lives what they will? He found that not only do his clients suffer from the trials of being human, but they also suffer from believing they have only themselves to blame for them. With success comes self-congratulation; with failure comes self-castigation.

Like everything else in its wake, neoliberalism casts sexism and racism in individual and private terms. Bruce Rogers-Vaughn says, "Neither is believed by dominant interests to have *structural* origins, but supposedly appear only in the behaviors of *individual* bigots and chauvinists."[21] Furthermore, "the answer to prejudice and discrimination is no longer social justice or systemic change, but psychotherapy, rehabilitation, or incarceration."[22] According to another writer in the field of pastoral theology, Cedric C. Johnson, "racialized neoliberalism" has created a "traumatogenic environment" for Blacks, and he thus uses trauma theory to respond to its harmful effects.[23] He also writes of neoliberalism's permeation of the will and the psyche: "Neoliberal hegemony governs disenfranchised groups through containment and control, but predominantly by

---

20. Bruce Rogers-Vaughn, *Care for Souls in a Neoliberal Age* (London: Palgrave Macmillan, 2016). See also Ryan LaMothe, *Pastoral Reflections on Global Citizenship: Framing the Political in Terms of Faith, Care, and Community* (London: Lexington, 2018); and LaMothe, "Neoliberal Capitalism and the Corruption of Society: A Pastoral Political Analysis," *Pastoral Psychology* 65, no. 1 (2016): 5–21, https://doi.org/10.1007/s11089-013-0577-x.

21. Bruce Rogers-Vaughn, "Powers and Principalities: Initial Reflections toward a Postcapitalist Pastoral Theology," *Journal of Pastoral Theology* 25, no. 2 (December 2015): 82, https://doi.org/10.1179/1064986715Z.00000000010 (emphasis mine).

22. Rogers-Vaughn, 82.

23. Cedric Johnson, *Race, Religion, and Resilience in the Neoliberal Age* (New York: Palgrave Macmillan, 2016), 85.

transforming them into subjects who voluntarily embrace particular kinds of choices and behaviors."[24]

Neoliberal ways of thinking have affected communal entities such as families, faith communities, neighborhoods, schools, and civic associations. The radical individualism of neoliberalism has diminished the reach and power of communal entities, and furthermore, their values and inner workings have been co-opted by individualism, commodification, and competition characteristic of neoliberal ways of arranging human relationships.[25] Neoliberal principles have infiltrated areas beyond the economy. According to Miguel De La Torre, "Neoliberalism tends to encompass and dictate every aspect of human existence. Nothing can exist outside the market. . . . Each thing and every body is reduced to a consumer good."[26] Neoliberalism infects social entities in order to "*maintain conditions* for unfettered markets and to *clean up* financial collapses, eco-messes, and regional conflicts created by that collusion."[27]

The effects of neoliberalism are manifest in Durham in several ways. *Low wage jobs* have shifted to other countries and no longer provide stable employment, as happened with the departure of tobacco jobs from Durham. Around the same time, during the neoliberal Reagan administration years, federal expenditure on public housing and housing vouchers "dropped from $26 billion to $8 billion," exacerbating the impact of these job losses.[28] Fortunately, one

---

24. Johnson, 49.
25. Rogers-Vaughn, *Care for Souls*, 72–78.
26. Miguel De La Torre, "Interfaith Relations and the Pursuit of Justice," *Review and Expositor* 114, no. 1 (2017): 81, https://doi.org/10.1177/0034637316687358.
27. William E. Connolly, *The Fragility of Things: Self-Organizing Processes, Neoliberal Fantasies, and Democratic Activism* (Durham, NC: Duke University Press, 2013), 20 (emphasis mine). Similarly, Walter Brueggemann draws parallels between empire in the history of Israel and the current imperialist thrust of the United States. Each nation is characterized by "extraction," a movement of wealth from the poor to the wealthy, and "commoditization," where "everything and everyone [is] reduced to a dispensable commodity that [can] be bought and sold and traded and possessed and consumed." Finally, these empires are willing to use violence to preserve this extraction and commoditization. Brueggemann, *God, Neighbor, Empire: The Excess of Divine Fidelity and the Command of Common Good* (Waco, TX: Baylor University Press, 2016), 2.
28. Chris Roberts, "The Great Eliminator: How Reagan Made Homelessness Permanent," *San Francisco Weekly*, June 29, 2016, https://tinyurl.com/y34fmjen.

of Durham's mayors, Wib Gulley, led an effort to pass two bond issues on affordable housing during the years 1986–89.

Cuts in funds for social services have produced increases in the number of people living in extreme poverty levels all over the country, and Durham has not escaped its effects. These cuts are based on policy instituted in the mid-1990s. Before 1996, under the sixty-year-old Aid to Families with Dependent Children (AFDC), families living in poverty were eligible to receive cash assistance along with food stamps, housing assistance, and medical care. In 1996, President Bill Clinton discontinued AFDC and promised to "end welfare as we know it." It was replaced with Temporary Assistance for Needy Families (TANF). A five-year lifetime limit for receiving aid as well as work requirements was instituted with the hope that welfare recipients would be able to find work to support themselves instead of receiving cash from the government. However, viable jobs were not forthcoming, and by 2011, more than twice the number of people in the United States were living in extreme poverty.[29] Working families did better; they benefited from the Earned Income Tax Credits, especially families living just above or just below the poverty line. Four years after the beginning of TANF, the number of children living in extreme poverty was 1.9 million; today it is 2.7 million.[30] A United Nations document states that the United States' "immense wealth and expertise stand in shocking contrast with the conditions in which vast numbers of its citizens live."[31] The report goes on to say that "5.3 million [Americans] live in *Third World conditions of absolute poverty.*"[32]

---

29. Kathryn J. Edin and H. Luke Shaeffer, *$2 a Day: Living on Almost Nothing in America* (Boston: Houghton Mifflin, 2015), xvii.

30. "Chart Book: Temporary Assistance for Needy Families," Center on Budget and Policy Priorities, accessed November 11, 2011, https://tinyurl.com/y2urbj38.

31. "Report of the Special Rapporteur on Extreme Poverty and Human Rights on His Mission to the United States of America," Human Rights Council, thirty-eighth session, June 18–July 6, 2018, http://undocs.org/A/HRC/38/33/ADD.1.

32. Jessica L. Semega, Kayla R. Fontenot, and Melissa A. Kollar, "Income and Poverty in the United States: 2016—Current Population Reports," US Census Bureau, September 2017, https://tinyurl.com/y7lat5gn (emphasis mine). See also Angus Deaton, "The U.S. Can No Longer Hide from Its Deep Poverty Problem," *New York Times*, January 24, 2018, https://tinyurl.com/yafsq9vx.

These dramatic increases in extreme poverty can be traced to the dramatic cuts in aid instituted in 1996.[33]

The lack of cash is often apparent at UMD. It is not at all rare for me to encounter people who have no money at all: not for a bus ticket, a cigarette, or a soft drink, and not for diapers, an identification card, or a medication copay. They simply have no cash at all. A painful moment was when a woman I knew stopped me as I was driving away from UMD. She asked me for some money, and when I said I do not carry cash, she asked if she could look on the floor of my car and in the crevices of the seat for spare change.

I spoke to Dan Hudgins, the director of Durham County Social Services for decades, about the effects of the end of AFDC and the implementation of TANF. He expressed strong criticism of TANF and gave me North Carolina figures that parallel Durham's experience. Before TANF, seventy-four out of every one hundred impoverished families with children in North Carolina received cash assistance. By 2015, only seven out of one hundred impoverished families received cash payments. In the same time period, the number of families in North Carolina who were living in deep poverty increased by 75 percent, while TANF was serving 85 percent fewer families.[34] The cuts in social services characteristic of neoliberalism have not served Durham's impoverished communities well.

The *privatization* of formerly publicly administered services, a feature of neoliberalism, has severely affected the delivery of mental health care in Durham. In North Carolina, county health departments had been responsible for mental health care services for years. The privatization of these services "destroyed" the local mental health system, according to one social services provider. Many of the UMD clients live with a serious mental illness, and I am often disturbed by the length of time to secure an initial appointment and the time between appointments.

---

33. For a robust analysis of the connection between TANF and neoliberal policy, see Joe Soss, Richard C. Fording, and Sanford Schram, *Disciplining the Poor: Neoliberal Paternalism and the Persistent Power of Race* (Chicago: University of Chicago Press, 2011).

34. "North Carolina's TANF Cash Assistance Is Disappearing for Poor Families," Center on Budget and Policy Priorities, accessed November 11, 2018, https://tinyurl.com/y258rjsb.

In addition to the privatization of mental health services, low-income housing has taken a turn toward privatization. While many imagine a large-scale public housing project when they hear of subsidized housing, many Durham residents rely on Section 8 housing vouchers, or Housing Choice vouchers. Under this program, low-income tenants pay a fraction of the market rate for a privately owned rental unit while public funds make up the rest of the rent. This shift to more and more vouchers for low-income housing is a form of privatization of the affordable housing supply. I have seen two great disadvantages to the voucher system: long waiting lists for vouchers, up to two years, and difficulty finding landlords who will accept housing vouchers. Thus after a person seeking housing finally receives a voucher after a long wait, they have a hard time finding a place to use it. Privatization has not solved the affordable housing crisis in Durham.

The close relation of the *criminal justice system* and *poverty* hides the impoverishing effects of neoliberal policies from the general public. It is harder to mobilize public opinion around poverty solutions when so many impoverished people are hidden in jails and prisons. It has also been argued that the results of neoliberal policies—increasing inequality and increased numbers trapped at the lowest rung of society—require greater policing and incarceration as a form of social control. Increases in incarceration serve to "contain the disorders produced by mass unemployment, the imposition of precarious wage work and the shrinking of social protection."[35]

The way the criminal justice system is connected to the consequences of neoliberal economic policies is evident in the lives of the people at the shelter when the jail becomes a backup for neoliberalism's inadequate social safety net. The largest deliverer of mental health services is the Durham County jail.[36] I remember the man who considered committing a crime so he could stay in jail on a cold night. I remember the desperate social worker who hoped a client would be arrested so that he could get emergency mental health

---

35. Loïc Wacquant, "The Penalisation of Poverty and the Rise of Neo-liberalism," *European Journal on Criminal Policy and Research* 9, no. 4 (2001): 401, https://doi.org/10.1023/A:1013147404519.

36. Dan Hudgins, face-to-face personal communication, June 13, 2018.

care. I see people just released from jail who look cleaner, healthier, and more rested than usual because basic human needs for food, shelter, hygiene, and health care were met in ways they were denied while living without a home.

There are fewer *social entities* to provide identity, purpose, and other forms of social capital. Neoliberalism has eroded social entities that provided emotional support and sources of meaning for many. I have heard many accounts of "back in the day" when whole neighborhoods looked after the children and youth, providing a meal when they were hungry and calling them to account when they were acting out. Now I hear of parents keeping children inside for fear they will become entangled in "the wrong crowd." I see window shades kept drawn all day to decrease visibility to those who might want to do harm. I hear of older people no longer sitting on the front porch because of the possibility of stray bullets coming from a passing car. As children, church attendance used to be mandatory for many I have spoken with—"My grandmama made me"—but now they see children growing up unchurched. Charter schools, magnet schools, and private schools have weakened Durham's neighborhood schools as sources of social cohesion. Businesses, restaurants, a movie theater, and a hotel that were all destroyed by the freeway reduced access to regular public meeting places. As neoliberalism's negative effects on sociality have grown throughout the globe, Durham is not exempt.

People living in poverty in Durham have been directly affected by national and global economic neoliberal trends. I would have expected that our small city would be only slightly touched by the world economy as it leans toward a particular economic and governing philosophy. However, the effects of neoliberalism are clearly seen in my city and the people I serve at UMD.

The Wounds of Poverty

Poverty alters the experience of time and space. Sam was staying at UMD because in order to be approved for disability payments, he had to have five drug tests per week for two months, and they had to be administered in Durham. When asked how long he would be here, he said, "I'm here for two clean urines!" Time is measured in urine test results. The time to get to work is measured in the number of bus transfers, and time is passed in the library, bus station, or riding a bus circuit.

Space is altered as well. The dumpster is transformed from a place of refuse to a place to find a meal. The restroom in McDonald's is a humbling place for a bath. One woman staying at UMD said other women in the dorm were acting superior to her. She told us, "Those other girls need to remember times when they had to wash their butts in McDonald's; they can't say they haven't." A secluded stand of trees in the city becomes a home. The waiting room at the emergency department becomes a sheltered place for the night, or hospital rooms for people living with HIV/AIDS become a place to rest and take a bath.

Homelessness is inherently a problem of embodiment.[37] A home enables a *safe* body, a body safe from guns, from physical attacks. Homeless women sleeping outside are vulnerable to rape, theft, and murder. A home allows for a *clean* body. It offers a place to get clean, to observe conventions of hygiene. The daily cluster of people waiting at one end of the UMD café for showers may be sleeping outside and may not have showered in days. A home provides a *sheltered* body. It is a place to retreat from heat, cold, rain, and snow. Bodies need warmth. A home makes for a *locatable* body. It provides a mailing address, a place where your family can find you, where an employer can send a check. It is a place to receive a disability payment and Christmas and birthday cards. A home provides for an *eating and drinking* body. It is a place to store food and to prepare it, to keep the milk cold and to cook up some dinner. Without a home, all food has to be bought ready to eat, which means fast food or packaged food. A home is a place for a *convalescing* body. It is a place to recover when ill or after surgery. It is a place to die. A home is a place for a *temporal* body. It provides a place to keep childhood photos and keepsakes, which mark time. It is a place to store papers validating origins, accomplishments, and

---

37. For a fascinating exploration of the effects of warfare, natural disaster, refugee status, American life without shelter, and the experience of PTSD as forms of "forced displacement," see M. Jan Holton, *Longing for Home: Forced Displacement and Postures of Hospitality* (New Haven, CT: Yale University Press, 2016), esp. 135–65.

identity. It is a place to keep off-season clothes. Safe, clean, sheltered, locatable, eating and drinking, convalescing, temporal bodies need homes.

I asked one young woman where she and her friend slept during the five years they did not have a home. She said,

———

Everywhere. I slept, for a while, there's a door out here, when you go out the cafeteria, I slept there for a while, like on nights that it rained. I slept across the street against that fence on that sidewalk. I slept by city hall on the little cut when it rained. I slept in the elevator shaft. I really wasn't an abandoned house person because I was kind of scared—you know, police. You know, so I slept in an abandoned house maybe twice, maybe once or twice. I stayed, you know, couch hopping, just a whole bunch of different things. . . . It was rough. It was cold, because we slept outside in all elements, whether it was raining, sleeting, snowing, hot, real cold. It'd be so cold that you in the sleeping bag and when you get up in the morning, your body imprint from the heat that your body has. And that's how cold it is outside—that your body print is on the concrete. Yeah, it was rough, but I got through it, so I knew then that if I could do that, I can do anything. Especially being here in Durham and a lot of people just getting killed for no reason, it was kind of scary on that aspect, like, "OK, well I hope nobody don't come and try to rob us because we don't got nothing but some blankets."[38]

———

This condition of homelessness is not unlivable. People do live without stable housing for years. Nor is extreme poverty unlivable. Yet living without a home, and living in extreme poverty, *increases the proximity* to what I will call "horror." I don't see horror often, certainly not every time I am at the shelter. But *horror hovers.* Life in extreme poverty is not one of unmitigated wretchedness; horror is

---

38. Today, this young woman is in her own apartment with her two children after having completed two programs for families and individuals. She is very skilled in computers and other forms of technology.

not a description of what life is like every moment. But horror does describe a *universe of ever-impinging possibilities*; it describes what always remains a potentiality. The lived reality of extreme poverty is a world where boundaries of protection, safety, dignity, wholeness, and health are often broken. And once a broken boundary has been experienced once, or five times, or a hundred times, the thought that it may be broken again is always there; in other words, horror hovers. When one experiences living without shelter, there are far fewer reliable boundaries between horror, self, and body. If a wound is a rupture of the body's boundary, skin, then we can also understand poverty is a great wound of the body, mind, and spirit. Three sources of suffering while living without a home are violence, being "on the street," and the abandonment of people living with serious mental illness.

Violence

The boundary of bodily safety is broken by violence.[39]

Violence against women. A woman looking distressed, rubbing her neck, saying her boyfriend tried to kill her. Two of us prayed with her in the parking lot. She is still with him. I know him fairly well. I have always been glad to see him. I once had two women in my office who had been raped, one within the last few weeks, the other years ago. One of them asked me to get her adult Depends because she was still bleeding. The other said she remembered the ongoing bleeding after her rape. They commiserated.

Violence between women. It was a Christmas party, and there was a commotion on the other side of the church assembly hall. I thought there was a fire. There were crashing sounds, screams, chairs falling over. A small boy was crying on the edges, and someone kindly picked him up.

Violence between men. I had never heard the sounds of two men fighting before. Bodies were thudding against each other, not

---

39. Sexual violence, gun violence, and intimate partner violence are not limited to people living in poverty. Deep-seated misogyny and racism, widespread patriarchal structures, a culture in love with guns, and a nation born in violence contribute to violent acts in all strata of American life.

a slapping sound, more of a thumping sound. It was louder than I expected. The power of two bodies directed against each other.

Violence against children. I watched a toddler, about two years old, in a stroller as I talked to her mother. The little girl has a sexually transmitted disease that flares up with fluid oozing from her "p———," her grandmother told me. Men in the substance abuse recovery program told me of the sexual violence they endured as boys.

These forms of violence can be called "direct violence," bodily harm in the form of murder, rape, knifing, physically damaging another. It is the most visible form of violence, and it is what I have witnessed and heard about at the shelter. However, direct violence occurs in the context of "structural violence," the unjust social, economic, legal institutions that deprive others of well-being and access to the means of human flourishing. "Affliction is embedded" in unjust social and economic systems.[40] Poverty itself is a form of violence.[41] There is a third form of violence that normalizes both direct and structural violence: "cultural violence." Deeply engrained racism—which normalized slavery, lynching, and police brutality—and the broad acceptance of persistent, extreme poverty are forms of cultural violence.[42] The acts of direct violence that I witness or

---

40. Paul Farmer, "An Anthropology of Structural Violence," *Current Anthropology* 45, no. 3 (2004): 305, https://www.jstor.org/stable/10.1086/382250. Elsewhere, Paul Farmer and Barbara Rylko-Bauer give this full definition of structural violence: "Structural violence is the violence of injustice and inequity. . . . By structures we mean social relations and arrangements—economic, political, legal, religious, or cultural—that shape how individuals and groups interact within a social system. These include broad-scale cultural and political-economic structures such as caste, patriarchy, slavery, apartheid, colonialism, and neoliberalism, as well as poverty and discrimination by race, ethnicity, gender, sexual orientation, and migrant/refugee status. These structures are violent because they result in avoidable deaths, illness, and injury; and they reproduce violence by marginalizing people and communities, constraining their capabilities and agency, assaulting their dignity, and sustaining inequalities." Farmer and Rylko-Bauer, "Structural Violence, Poverty, and Social Suffering," in *The Oxford Handbook of the Social Science of Poverty*, ed. David Brady and Linda M. Burton (Oxford: Oxford University Press, 2016), 48.

41. Josephine A. V. Allen, "Poverty as a Form of Violence: A Structural Perspective," *Journal of Human Behavior in the Social Environment* 4, no. 2/3 (2001): 45–59, https://doi.org/10.1300/J137v04n02_03. Allen says that "poverty is one of the deadliest forms of violence" (45).

42. Johan Galtung, "Cultural Violence," *Journal of Peace Research* 27, no. 3 (1990): 295, https://www.jstor.org/stable/423472.

hear described must be understood in the context of both cultural and structural violence.[43]

There are risks in writing about violence among people living in extreme poverty. It may "otherize" them, suggesting that violence is confined to those with low or no incomes. Or it could suggest there is a lack of control or civility among people who live in poverty. It also contributes to the association of Black people with criminality. I try to mitigate that risk by including in this portrayal of life in poverty the ordinary, the good, the faithful, the wise, the honorable, the generous, and the lovely. Another risk is suggesting that personal moral failure or an intrinsic drive toward aggression and violence is responsible for the higher rates of violence under conditions of poverty. This risk is illustrated in some writing on poverty in America that depicts zones of poverty using the term *underclass*, which problematically "evoked *a territory full of violence and despair* . . . [and] a gendered image of urban poverty, frightening Americans with the menace posed by black men and alarming them with the passivity of black women who avoided work, birthed illegitimate children, and lived on the charity of the welfare state."[44] I want to avoid creating a picture of the "mysterious, menacing, pathogenic, and isolated districts at the core of American cities."[45] The challenge is to tell the truth about suffering and its sources without dehumanizing the place and its inhabitants.

"On the Street"

Sometimes "on the street" simply means living outside, or in an abandoned building, or in a cubbyhole, as one person called the place where he slept. Some emphasize the social disconnection of being on the street. One man with a full head of white hair and a thick white beard said, "It means losing your family and everybody else you need. At my age, my birthday today, I'm seventy-six; it's just a lonely thing." Another older man echoed his thoughts:

---

43. See the essay that first proposed the concept of "structural violence": Johan Galtung, "Violence, Peace, and Peace Research," *Journal of Peace Research* 6, no. 3 (1969): 167–91, https://www.jstor.org/stable/422690. See also Farmer, "Anthropology of Structural Violence," 305.
44. Katz, *Undeserving Poor*, 205 (emphasis mine).
45. Katz, 206.

"It's terrible. Lonely. Nobody to turn to. Homeless. I been that way since I was fifteen."

To others, "on the street" refers to "nothing but sex, money, and drugs," as one person said with increasing intense anger. It can mean a life catering to a substance use disorder, which may result in having sex for money, selling illegal drugs, or theft.

Life in extreme poverty on the streets literally kills. People in deep poverty die young. One woman I met was talking about her health problems, and I noticed her arm was in a sling. She was tall and wearing a scarf around her head that had released a few tufts of hair. She had the appearance of solidity and strength. She was hesitant but alert. I asked her if she had just had surgery, and she said, "Yes, they went in and removed fifteen spurs and scraped her down to the bone."

"Did you play a lot of sports?"

"Yes, but you can't live homeless for twenty-seven years and not get something wrong with your body," she shot back as if I were willfully clueless to a core human truth.

"That is a long time . . ."

"I was gang-raped by six guys, one after the other."[46] These words were popping out fiercely, loudly, fast, with much energy behind them. She testified to the inscription of poverty on her female body. Her body wore poverty.[47]

The untimely death of people in poverty has been tolerated for generations. Their deaths are "ungrievable," meaning their lives and deaths are considered inconsequential, unworthy of notice, outside the realm of full humanity.[48] "Who counts as human? Whose lives count as lives? And, finally, *What makes for*

---

46. I don't mean to suggest that gang rape is confined to poverty. My point is that her unhoused female body is vulnerable to violence.

47. Anthony Pinn says, "Regarding the literal *wearing of poverty*, the physical health and carriage of the body are harmed as poverty-related illnesses destroy its integrity. In a sense, poverty 'erases' the physical body through progressive deterioration caused by poor diet and inadequate health care." Pinn, "Warm Bodies, Cold Currency: A Study of Religion's Response to Poverty," in *Religion and Poverty: Pan-African Perspectives*, ed. Peter J. Paris (Durham, NC: Duke University Press, 2009), 235.

48. Judith Butler, *Precarious Life: The Powers of Mourning and Violence* (London: Verso, 2004), 20.

the grievable life?[49] These questions could also be asked about the lives of people who die in extreme poverty by the intertwining direct, structural, and cultural violence. Of course, there is grief among families of people dead through any means, including violence, deprivation, or chronic lack. Indeed, families, neighborhoods, communities are often in a state of chronic grief over losses they have suffered. Claudia Rankine's article entitled "The Condition of Black Life Is One of Mourning" refers to this pervasive sorrow.[50] The term *ungrievable* highlights our national blindness, numbness, indifference to certain deaths because the people who died were not considered fully human in the first place. A certain number of deaths among people living in poverty are tolerated, and it is far from the focus of national effort to mitigate their occurrence.

In the Prayer Service, we have mourned many people who were participants in our community: a young woman who was murdered, a woman who stepped in front of a train, a young man and a young woman with uncontrolled diabetes, a man who was HIV positive and died young, and several formerly unhoused people who were found dead in their homes after years of homelessness. These deaths are often invisible and unnoteworthy to the larger world. In order for the world to mourn the loss of a person, "there would have to have been a life, a life worth noting, a life worth valuing and preserving, a life that qualifies for recognition," and so often this is not the case for people without homes.[51]

Serious Mental Illness: Abandonment

Our system of care for people with serious mental illness is a national disgrace, and one manifestation of this is the "institutional

49. Butler, 20. Butler first asked these questions about the civilian dead in recent wars waged by the United States, then she draws into this category the young Black men shot by the police. She says, "The callous killing of Tamir Rice and the abandonment of his body on the street is an astonishing example of the police murdering someone considered disposable and fundamentally ungrievable." George Yancy and Judith Butler, "What's Wrong with All Lives Matter?," *New York Times*, January 12, 2015, https://tinyurl.com/yyctbd7r.
50. Claudia Rankine, "The Condition of Black Life Is One of Mourning," *New York Times*, June 22, 2015, https://tinyurl.com/y79ug5rd.
51. Butler, *Precarious Life*, 34.

circuit," in which people with serious mental illness cycle through homelessness, jail, the state mental hospital, and the homeless shelter. An example of this path might be the following: A person is living outside and then arrested while intoxicated for public urination or trespassing and taken to jail. The jail releases them to the homeless shelter, but soon, the shelter is unable to manage symptoms of mental illness and sends the person for a mental health assessment, and the person is admitted to a state psychiatric hospital. Eventually, the person is released from the hospital, but they are unable to manage without support, and they find themselves in jail again. The cycle begins again. This pattern characterizes many people at UMD who sometimes appear at the shelter after a period in jail, or in the psychiatric hospital, or living without a home only to move on to the next stop on the circuit.[52]

Ever since I started at the shelter ten years ago, a young man has eaten, showered, and hung out there. His name is Charles, and he is very quiet, and though I see him talking to himself softly and occasionally smiling, I have never seen him talk to anyone. He illustrates the vivid category "zone of social abandonment," especially apt for many unsheltered people living with serious mental illness.[53] In Durham, we do not have spatial zones, but we have social zones of abandonment, which Charles occupies. Equally heartbreaking are the people who receive all that the safety net can give: subsidized housing, a disability check, food stamps, mental health care. They may even seek church membership and participation in a faith community and be a regular participant. Yet still, *still*, they remain outside the bonds of human affection and mutual support, outside the warmth of a community of peers who miss them when they are absent, who remember to share a story meant just for them, who notice when they are having a bad day. One such person is Eddie.

Eddie was tall and fit and always wore knee pads. He had worked as a laborer with the same crew for fifteen years and

---

52. See J. Jost et al., "Homelessness, Severe Mental Illness, and the Institutional Circuit," *Psychiatric Services* 48, no. 5 (1997): 659–64.

53. João Biehl, *Vita: Life in a Zone of Social Abandonment* (Berkeley: University of California Press, 2013). Biehl writes of an asylum in Porto Alegre, Brazil, named Vita for people who live with serious mental illness and who have been completely abandoned by family and friends. They are brought there to die.

had developed a solid community with his coworkers and was especially connected to his boss. He worked hard and even went to work on "weather days." Then because of his "disorder," he had to leave his job. Though I don't know for sure, I believe the emergence of a mental disorder led to him losing his job. Both of his parents have died, and he desperately wanted another job. "Otherwise," he says, "I just walk around. If I stay at home, I feel walls closing in on me." He "gave his life to the Lord" some years ago, and he prays and studies the Bible at home. "I stay in the book of Mark. That's where I live at," he says. He fasts for twenty-four hours once a week. When I asked how God helps him, he said, "I eat proper foods, drink lots of water. When I read the word of God, I buy proper food. He shows me patience, how not to get mad and to give it to him. [I gave] him thanks this morning, [asked him to] guide me, direct me in the right path. And I keep giving it to him."

Church was a place where he hoped he would fulfill a meaningful purpose. He said, "I want to go to church so I can be a tool. I want to bring somebody to the house of God." Yet he has not felt welcome at any church. "People say there is something wrong with me. I try to stay focused and keep my mind on God. People say things, and I just give it to the Lord, go on about my business. I tried to be a member of a church, and that church don't want me there." It bothered him that nobody invited him to Bible study or said, "Glad you are here," not even the minister.

However, he goes to the gym regularly, saying, "Oh man, the gym is a big relief for me. I feel so good. At the gym, people say I work out like I'm going out for the football team." He gets a disability check, he gets his medication regularly by injection, his mental health benefits pay for his gym membership, and he has free time to walk around town. However, he is desperately missing the community, respect, and purpose that work and church membership offer. It seems that his job and the gym have been the most redemptive places for him as a person living with a serious mental illness, not a church. Many people living with serious mental illness receive all that the social services safety net provides, yet they still occupy the "zone of social abandonment." There is so much more to the care for people with serious mental illness than a check and a place to live. They also crave work, purpose, respect, and community.

Horror Impinges but Does Not Prevail

Of course, life in and around the shelter is not unmitigated horror, but horror remains in memories and is borne in bodies and displayed on bodies. In this context, people at the shelter practice their faith. They utter prayers for themselves, for each other, for their families. They read Scripture, especially the Psalms, from tattered Bibles. They wear crosses made of metal, wood, or string, some plain and some ornate, some bearing Jesus's body and some empty. They offer each other encouragement, companionship, humor, cigarettes, and spare change. One such moment of encouragement happened in the Prayer Service.

Randall listened while Tammy prayed and started to cry in the Prayer Service because she believed her large body size was responsible for the absence of a loving man in her life. The whole room was moved by her tears. She had been coming regularly, and we knew her well. We had heard of her mother's extraordinary cruelty toward her as a girl, and we were only now learning of this particular sorrow. When she was finished speaking, Randall spoke first. He said he understood. He felt most women don't see him as a real man because one of his legs was amputated. His words communicated empathy and kindness.

Later, in an interview, he explained the motivation for his kindness: "Because I can feel what she's feeling. . . . I'm always thinking I'm not with anyone because no one wants me because I don't have but one leg. No one wants me anymore. 'You handicapped,' lot of times I get that. So I know how she's feeling."

I pushed some more. "Why did you decide to be kind?"

"Because I feel I'm in the same boat that she's in."

"But you still didn't have to be kind."

"I've eat rat poison. I've did all of that over what people tell me. Even when I seen my own family. When I was in a wheelchair, 'Can I go with y'all guys shopping?' And they tell me, 'No we don't have room for your wheelchair.' [I thought at that time,] 'I don't want to live like this. What is the use?' I know how she was feeling at that moment."

Randall's favorite Bible verse, which he quoted often, was 2 Corinthians 1:3–4 (ESV): "Blessed be the God and Father of our Lord Jesus Christ, the Father of mercies and God of all comfort, who comforts us in all our affliction, *so that we may be able to comfort those who are in any affliction*, with the comfort with which we ourselves are comforted by God" (emphasis mine).

The Prayer Service provides a platform for speaking and enacting a world of comfort and grace in the midst of the horror that hovers in memories and bodies as well as an ever-present possibility in the present. Brutal, intractable horror is never far away, but there is respite; there is a witness to the persistence of grace, to a light that cannot be extinguished. We comfort the afflicted, grieve for the ungrievable, and offer each other good news.

The Prayer Service is also a space that refuses to let hell have the last word. James is in his seventies and usually wears a hat, baggy suit, and multiple IDs and tags around his neck. He almost always brings a stack of flyers about an upcoming community event, or he stands in the front making announcements about them. It might be a church health fair. It might be a community barbecue. It could be a workshop on finding housing. He is known among staff for his purveyance of announcements of community events of interest. He has done it for years.

We were about halfway through the Prayer Service when we were reminded of a prayer request from a woman who asked for prayers in the wake of the violent death of her cousin. James brought up another murder, and Missionary Richey added a story about a young man who had just been shot the night before. He had fled to his grandmother's house to escape gunshots. As he was pounding on her door, he was shot dead. His grandmother did not open the door, because she was afraid. The horrific reality of three recent, local murders hung in the air.

Then James got up with his flyers, saying, "We need some good news," and he handed everyone a flyer about a health fair and a church cookout. His good news was material, specific, and local: barbecued chicken and potato salad and iced tea at this address, at this time, offered by this church. Blood pressure measurements and diabetes tests at the fairgrounds on Cooper Road next Saturday, 9 a.m.–5 p.m. The gospel takes shape in material form within time and space. The good news is not in the form of a propositional statement but is material, specific, and local. The blind see, the lame walk, the lepers are cleansed, a free fish dinner is served at Heaven's Love Church at five o'clock this Sunday.

CHAPTER 2

FORM MATTERS

Harvey looked stricken as he finished his breakfast. The high ceiling in the former basketball court that now serves as the homeless shelter café only reinforced how small he looked as I approached him. He is a Black man in his sixties, and he speaks with a significant speech impediment. He pulled out a funeral worship bulletin with a photo of a smiling young man on the cover and said that his nephew had just died in a fire. Moved by his distress, I did what I often do when I can't take the pain away: I invited him to the Prayer Service.

The Prayer Service

I brought Harvey into the heart of my chaplaincy: the Prayer Service. It creates another world at Urban Ministries of Durham (UMD), offers an alternative space in the midst of the challenges of homelessness, or life on the street, or simply the strain of extreme poverty. We meet three mornings a week for half an hour. The original vision for this service was influenced by several sources. One influence was Killian Noe's book on establishing the Samaritan Inn in Washington, DC, where centering prayer was a central part of the substance abuse recovery program.[1] It served as

---

1. Killian Noe, *Finding Our Way Home: Addictions and Divine Love* (Scottsdale, PA: Herald Press, 2003). Thanks to Denise Thorpe for this reference.

an example of how a classical spiritual discipline can be adopted by people from vastly different religious traditions. Another influence was Oliver Sacks's *Musicophilia: Tales of Music and the Brain*, where he speaks of the power of music to reach past the cognitive and to evoke transcendence and realities beyond the visible.[2] This original vision called for time, space, and music for prayer and lighting candles. I pictured dim lighting, soft and meditative piano music, and a small group of people sitting with eyes closed and head bowed. In my imagination, people would walk forward intermittently to light a candle and say something like, "Healing for my mother" or "I pray for my kids."

However, instead of my contemplative model, people have brought their own forms of religion to the space I initiated. Rather than soft music punctuated by an occasional three-word prayer, people brought testimonies to what God has done. People brought short sermons on the moral life. People brought songs sung a cappella, and people brought the stories of their lives. It has become the place for writing lives in the idiom of the predominant religious forms of the area: southern Evangelicalism, mostly as it is lived in Black churches.

I share the leadership of the Prayer Service with Missionary Richey and Deacon Jack. I met Jack when I was walking past the long line of people waiting for lunch at UMD, and I heard a booming voice announce, "The only clergyman to sign the Declaration of Independence was a Presbyterian." He is a voracious consumer of information and shares it often with us. After finding who made the declaration, I saw Jack smiling. He has been a member of the Prayer Service from the beginning, moving into a leadership role after a couple of years, even after moving into permanent housing. What is most significant about his leadership is the small blue plastic box for holding 3" × 5" index cards that he brings to every service. He records the name of every new person at the service, and their name goes into the box. Anyone who attends the Prayer Service knows that when they leave UMD, we will continue to remember them and pray for them. Both he and Missionary Richey will start singing, and if it is familiar, everyone joins in.

---

2. Oliver Sacks, *Musicophilia: Tales of Music and the Brain* (New York: Knopf, 2007).

At the beginning of my work at UMD, I met Missionary Richey when she stopped by my office and introduced herself. As she tells the story, she saw the sign on my door that said chaplain and said to herself, "Chaplain. They work for God. I want to work with her." She has been a leader ever since. She serves as a song leader, consultant, and skilled bearer of Scripture texts.

When people go forward to "light a candle, say a prayer," as our publicity says, many times they simply say they want to pray for a place to live, for a job, for patience to live in the shelter dorm, for their recovery from addiction, for their children in foster care or prison or living with their relatives. They pray for their health, for their enemies, for others who are caught in addiction, for strength to withstand the devil. Very touching is a recitation of concern for the other worshippers who have passed through the Prayer Service community, even years earlier: "I saw Thomas on the bus, and he looked bad." "Georgia found a place to stay." "Let's pray for Marvin and Wilma and Henry and Tracy and . . ." The list can contain ten to fifteen names of people who are absent, who may have recently shared concerns in the service, or who may not have been seen for several years. The presence of saints, both in the room and absent, and their concerns echo in the Prayer Service room.

Between such offerings, there is music playing in the background as people quietly read a Bible or pray. There may be information shared about what time the Durham County Social Services opens, which bus route to take to the mall, or where an apartment is available, for example. There may be news of a knifing in the neighborhood. There may be statements connected to what has been said, such as "My Aunt used to get her hair done there" or "His cousin married a Jehovah's Witness." There may be a debate over whether the use of translations other than the King James Version should be used. The mundane, the tragic, and the sublime are all subjects of prayer, testimony, and discussion.

Other ways to nurture the spirit are offered to unhoused people around our country. Just down the street at the Rescue Mission, there is a very structured service that includes preaching and a clear distinction between the worship leader and the worshippers. Some groups offer outdoor worship in a downtown park or other urban space. There are mainline churches in Atlanta and Nashville that offer short worship services that include a brief homily and an order of worship.

In contrast, I was committed to a service where the words and forms were primarily generated by the people who eat and sleep at the shelter. What has emerged is a service with no sermon, no order of worship, and fluid and shared leadership. The Prayer Service is a place where people without homes who are chronically treated as "out of place" have the sense of being "in place"; it has become a zone of belonging and recognition.[3] As such, it has become not only a zone of belonging and recognition but a site of creativity and generativity. Unrecognizable instrumental music has shifted to recognizable instrumental hymn music that strikes familiar and grounding chords. In time, we added soft hymns with words, such as "Precious Lord" and "Amazing Grace." Finally, in response to statements such as "That music sounds like a funeral" and "People who come here are sad, and we need something to pick them up," livelier music was added from both traditional and contemporary gospel genres.

People bring the words, music, gestures, rhetoric, intonations, and rituals from their own heritage into the Prayer Service. Approximately 90 percent of participants are Black. They bring with them residues of their Black Church experience, which offers much more than familiarity. It "promotes the healing of harmed humanity, and the nurturing of a sense of beauty and 'fullness,' within the context of a world that does not readily see her or his importance."[4] Through these pieces of their religious heritage, through its healing, beauty, and fullness, participants are fed, and they participate in a "theological and ritual counter to the way in which oppressive forces destroy the integrity—both literally and figuratively—of the Black body."[5]

---

3. Tim Cresswell, *In Place / Out of Place: Geography, Ideology, and Transgression* (Minneapolis: University of Minnesota Press, 1996), 4. Speaking of New York in the eighties, Cresswell says, "Homelessness is treated as an instance of people out of place." Cresswell, 5. I am grateful to Cynthia Curtis for this insight.

4. Anthony Pinn, "Sweaty Bodies in a Circle: Thoughts on the Subtle Dimensions of Black Religion as Protest," *Black Theology: An International Journal* 4, no. 1 (2006): 12.

5. Pinn, 12.

Practical theologian Dale P. Andrews reminds us of the "refuge" function of many Black churches, and the Prayer Service approximates that function in some small way.[6] Some participants have referred to the difference between the hazards of life "out there" and the benefits of life "in here" at the Prayer Service. The Prayer Service is a place to be around "positive" people as opposed to "negative" people, it is said. One person said that people go to church to get away from "the hood," and the Prayer Service plays the role of church. Another person contrasted the Prayer Service world to the "cold world." He said,

------

[The Prayer Service] keeps me encouraged. I want a better life than feeling useless, hopeless. I need to be self-motivated. . . . I remember how hard it was sleeping outside. It's a cold world; people don't care.

The Prayer Service for many is a place where mood and outlook can change.

---

6. Dale P. Andrews, *Practical Theology for Black Churches: Bridging Black Theology and African American Folk Religion* (Louisville, KY: Westminster John Knox, 2002), 34. Here Andrews reminds us that the image originally came from E. Franklin Frazier's *The Negro Church in America* (New York: Schocken, 1963). Others have recognized the "priestly" function of the Black Church, which is concerned with worship and spirituality, and they place it in a "dialectic" relationship with the "prophetic" function of the Black Church. C. Eric Lincoln and Lawrence H. Mamiya, *The Black Church in the African American Experience* (Durham, NC: Duke University Press, 1990), 11. Gayraud Wilmore, Carroll Watkins Ali, and Homer Ashby note the intermingling of these two functions of the Black Church, disputing their relationship as "dialectic." See Wilmore, *Black Religion and Black Radicalism: An Interpretation of the History of Afro-American People*, 2nd ed. (Maryknoll, NY: Orbis, 1998); Watkins Ali, *Survival and Liberation: Pastoral Theology in African American Context* (St. Louis: Chalice, 1999); and Ashby, *Our Home Is over Jordan: A Black Pastoral Theology* (St. Louis: Chalice, 2003). For example, Ashby represents Wilmore's thought by saying, "Mere survival is a political act," combining a pastoral and an emancipatory function. Ashby, 36. Refuge, survival, and a priestly role all denote parts of the Black Church experience that is both one with and distinct from liberationist, prophetic, resisting functions of the Black Church.

———

- When I go in, I might be having an issue or something, so I'm not all that jolly about coming up in there. But once I come up in there, and service gets started, and everybody gets to sharing the candles, then I start to feel a certain way—this exactly what I needed.

- I walk in and I don't feel too good, but once I get in and sit down and stuff and hear the church music playing and we do our little candle lighting thing and people get up there, I feel good when I come out of there. I may not feel too good when I walk in, but when I come out of it, I feel good. I feel wonderful.

- I get a lot of encouragement from other people [at the Prayer Service] 'cause some people think, "I'm the only one going through this." No, I'm not the only one going through this or that. So a lot of people be going through some stuff, and then I learn something from them.

———

They describe what I hoped to offer Harvey that morning as he arrived at the Prayer Service.

As usual, the service began with someone going to the podium in the front of the room to bring their prayer concerns. Then Harvey went to the podium. His eyes filled with tears, and his face crinkled as he spoke. It was hard to understand his words, but we could tell that he was speaking of how close he was to his nephew, and he knew that this beloved young man was in a better place now. After pausing there for a while, he sat down.

People in the congregation were attentive but said nothing. The service could have continued on as usual, with another person rising to bring their concerns. But wanting to linger with Harvey's words, I immediately stood up before anyone else could. I quoted Scripture: "If we live, we live to the Lord . . ." I softly said something empathetic and affirmed our presence with him during this difficult time. I was choosing my words very carefully, wanting to honor both Harvey's pain and the support of the people gathered around him. I called upon all that I knew from years of teaching a class on grief to ministry students: don't make false promises; don't prematurely rush to comfort; don't offer platitudes; simply offer community, prayer, and presence. Harvey and the rest of the group listened attentively but silently.

After I sat down, a middle-aged Black man, Marvin, stood up, walked to the podium, and declared loudly and firmly, "Christians don't die; they just fall asleep." That immediately got Harvey's attention. Marvin continued to speak with great clarity about Harvey's nephew and the sure and certain truth that all was well with him as he rested in the arms of the Almighty. Harvey responded with smiles, vigorous nods, and verbal affirmation. When Marvin sat down after a couple of minutes, Harvey was smiling and said he felt better already.

Marvin's response was very different from mine. I wanted to honor Harvey and his sorrow by empathically articulating his feelings, and I wanted to affirm the presence of God in this community gathered around him. I did not want to ignore the desolation of the bereaved. I wanted Harvey to know that we were sitting at the foot of the cross with him, and we would not prematurely rush to resurrection in a way that ignored his pain. I offered responses from my academic and ecclesial world that are considered trustworthy ways of responding to the bereaved. In this context, however, my words left nothing but silence in their wake. By contrast, Marvin, who came after me, was preaching. He proclaimed God's resurrection power. He used well-worn sayings, familiar speech cadence, Scripture, facial expressions, body movement—all to communicate that death does not have the last word, that God is powerful, that Harvey's nephew's life is not over, that his life and death matter in the eyes and heart of God Almighty. Marvin and I differed on our sense of what was needed at the moment. I tried to sit in the silence of Harvey's broken heart and assure him of the presence of the gathered community. Marvin's preaching decisively brought Harvey to a place of reassurance in a style that appealed to the ear and the eye and to deep archives of religious memory.

Marvin and I brought different forms of power to Harvey in his sorrow. Marvin's power was obvious: the skilled use of language, content, and delivery that evoked the presence and power of the divine for Harvey. I had wielded my social power to create and sustain the Prayer Service in the first place and to steer the group's attention to Harvey and his sorrow, refusing to let the depth of his pain go unremarked. Both Marvin and I were using the powers we had to comfort the broken heart of an uncle in mourning. I had social and cultural capital; Marvin had "community cultural wealth" in the form of facility in a particular style of performing words of comfort.[7] It is not up to me to learn to speak in the way Marvin did. I will never be able to do it authentically. But I can bring the power I have to gather people who do have those gifts, and I can turn their attention to wounds that need tending.

While the Prayer Service space is usually a place of grace and peace, that is not always the case. One time I entered the large cafeteria on the way to the Prayer Service room and one of the staff asked with some urgency for help with a situation just outside the door to the service. I saw a woman who had been a regular participant in the Prayer Service, of whom I am very fond, a tall woman whose deep wrinkles around her eyes were white in the summer in contrast to her deeply tanned skin. Though she often stayed at the shelter, her ill-fitting clothes and matted hair bore the signs of living outside. She was in a heated conversation with the director of UMD, a security guard, and a Black staff person. She was loudly complaining that she was asked to leave by the staff person when she had merely stopped to chat with someone on the way to the Prayer Service. She was now incensed because she wasn't going to let "Black people control my life." The director, who is also Black, handled the situation well, but I was reminded that the Prayer Service was not peopled by saints.

A minute later, I walked into the Prayer Service, which had already started. One of the faithful attenders was standing up and yelling across the room at a woman who was well known for her incendiary comments. His yelling and raging continued as he walked toward her and the door. He talked about what he ought to do to her head and face and became more and more menacing. I stepped between him and the woman and asked him to leave.

---

7. Tara J. Yosso, "Whose Culture Has Capital? A Critical Race Theory Discussion of Community Cultural Wealth," *Race Ethnicity and Education* 8, no. 1 (2005): 69–91. Yosso challenges Bourdieu's notion of cultural capital, saying that there are forms of capital in marginalized communities that middle-class values do not include. The capacity to use a culturally specific form of embodied speech as a way to respond to suffering is one form of "community cultural wealth."

Finally, they both left. I tried to name for the remaining people what had happened, and we talked about it, prayed for God's peace, and concluded the service.

The next time we met, there was much discussion of the event, and I was curious to see how they interpreted it. Would they speak of it as an event of personal threat? Would this be seen as a matter of two bad actors? Would they ignore it or find it an unnoteworthy part of everyday life?

Most of the comments were about how the Prayer Service space is not the streets, and people should not bring the streets into this place.[8] They said, "If you want to act like that, don't come in here." There was a sense of indignation that this brief thirty-minute period had been invaded by forces from the outside. They repeatedly affirmed the distinction between inside and outside this space. They concluded that this was a place of prayer, where cell phones would be silenced, there would be no cross talk or interruptions, a certain decorum would be observed, and it should return to a time of peace and reflection. Their commitment to restoring a valued time and place was clear, and it was clear that its value lay in its distinction from the streets.[9]

These two disconnected events that happened within minutes of each other were highly unusual. But they did serve as a reminder of the precariousness of the peace and refuge of the Prayer Service, that it should not be taken for granted, that it has to be nurtured and protected. This was a place of sanctuary, and participants were committed to maintaining it as such.

---

8. Timothy Nelson reports that the duality of church and street represents "all the other polarities—belief and unbelief, holiness and sin, salvation and damnation—that ultimately derive from the opposition between God and Satan." This observation underscores what is at stake in protecting sacred space from the street: it is about a great cosmic battle. Nelson, *Every Time I Feel the Spirit: Religious Experience and Ritual in an African American Church* (New York: New York University Press, 2005), 103.

9. Elijah Anderson reported a similar distinction in *Code of the Street: Decency, Violence, and the Moral Life of the Inner City* (New York: W. W. Norton, 1999). He wrote about the contrast between "decent" and "street" families. This perspective was roundly criticized by Loïc Wacquant in "Scrutinizing the Street: Poverty, Morality, and the Pitfalls of Urban Ethnography," *American Journal of Sociology* 107, no. 6 (May 2002): 1468–532. Wacquant says of Anderson, he "dichotomizes ghetto residents into good and bad, 'decent' and 'street,' and makes himself the spokesman and advocate of the former." Wacquant, 1469.

VARIETIES OF FORMS

One of the factors that marks the time and place of the Prayer Service as a sanctuary is the use of particular forms of ritual language and style. Ritual forms are ultimately about bodies. They are embodied performances of what is hoped for, of what is condemned, of transformations toward desired ways of being in the world.[10] In the Prayer Service, these bodily performances include swaying, clapping, gesturing, and voices intentionally varied by cadence, volume, and pitch. I first noticed the importance of form when the Prayer Service had just been created. I had offered carefully crafted prayers that I hoped would confer hope, comfort, and courage. I spoke in prose paragraphs trying hard to give precise, empathic expression to both their trials and God's love and power. However, I quickly sensed that my words fell flat, while others' offerings of prayer and testimony received energetic responses from the rest of the group. Soon, I realized that, among other things, it had to do with genre; it had to do with my lack of familiarity with forms of rhetoric and style that were intrinsic to the message. My offerings were like a horse race announcer who might state in a matter-of-fact voice, "Now the horses are beginning the last part of the race," instead of shouting, "Down the stretch they come!" Genre opens up truths, worlds, emancipations, connections that mere delivery of content cannot. Marvin was able to offer words "keyed by cultural symbols and referents" so that Harvey might feel "more surrounded by [his] own cultural space" while dwelling in a place of dislocation, a homeless shelter.[11]

Several genres emerged in the Prayer Service.

Sayings and Proverbs

What first brought my attention to the importance of form were the handwritten and then photocopied pages distributed by Missionary Richey that were read with great interest and often folded

---

10. See Catherine Bell, "Ritual," in *The Blackwell Companion to the Study of Religion*, ed. Robert A. Segal (London: Blackwell, 2006), 397.
11. Sw. Anand Prahlad, *African-American Proverbs in Context* (Jackson: University of Mississippi, 1996), 126.

and tucked away for future reference. These handouts included brief Scripture verses that are commonly heard in the service:

> We can do all things through Christ, who strengthens us.
>
> To be absent from the body is to be present with the Lord.
>
> No weapon formed against me shall prosper.
>
> Trust in the Lord with all your heart and soul; lean not unto your own understanding and he will direct your path.

Other sayings were nonscriptural proverbs familiar to many:

> God can do anything but fail.
>
> Don't let the devil steal your joy.
>
> Be good so you can be blessed.
>
> With God all things are possible.
>
> The devil is *real.*
>
> The devil is a liar.
>
> Count it all joy.
>
> I know he is able.
>
> Look at God.
>
> God is worthy to be praised.
>
> Acknowledge him in all thy ways.
>
> God got your back.

The force of these sayings no doubt came from deep memories of churchgoing and Scripture quoting from loved ones, as well as an archive of orally transmitted sayings that were in the cultural milieu of the shelter.[12] Proverbs bring "the original context in which the proverb was learned" as well as an "emotional psychological association . . . the basic psychological components of former context."[13] They are saturated with personal, ecclesial, and cultural history. Possibly,

---

12. Cleophus LaRue, *I Believe I'll Testify: The Art of African American Preaching* (Louisville, KY: Westminster John Knox, 2011), 135–38. LaRue includes a list of everyday sayings in a section on "Oral Formulas in the Black Culture."

13. Prahlad, *African-American Proverbs*, 126, 127.

they evoked memories of more stable times and of the community and beloved individuals from whom they first heard them. So much more than content was transmitted through them. The familiar proverbs and sayings also play a social role, as they function to bond the hearers in the Prayer Service to each other. Delivery of an apt and familiar saying to strangers who share a deep connection to the same originating archive establishes connections among them.

However, it was not only familiar proverbs that evoked responses but also new and unfamiliar sayings on these handouts that called forth positive responses, sayings such as

Do You Need to Have Some Repairs done? If so go to the Repairer Jesus, the Anointed One! He can fix anything.

Lets ask Jesus to be a fence around us.

A Word for the Devil! God got our back.

This suggests that the genre "saying" or "proverb" is as important as content. Genre and content combine to create the force of a saying. Not only familiar proverbs but also novel metaphors crafted into an *original proverb* are powerful forms of communication. My spoken paragraphs meant to convey meaning were far less effective than the wielding of sayings. I was witnessing the strength of sayings and proverbs to pass along "lessons and precepts about life and survival [that] are handed down from generation to generation."[14]

The endurance of these forms of speech is accounted for not by their effective transmission of inert deposits of rules and truths but rather in the genre's flexibility, its amenability to the creation of new content. Sayings and proverbs, testimony and sermon, are not simply lifeless units of truth. They are relational, used to interpret the words of someone who has spoken in the Prayer Service. They are wielded. Geneva Smitherman says, "The core strength of this tradition lies on its capacity to accommodate new situations and changing realities."[15] The skilled speaker can apply them to a variety of life's quandaries and pains and, furthermore, can even generate novel insight as a familiar saying meets a new situation. Thus the

---

14. Geneva Smitherman, *Talkin and Testifyin: The Language of Black America* (Boston: Houghton Mifflin, 1977), 73.
15. Smitherman, 73.

deployment of these sayings and proverbs, sermons and testimonies, is a form of doing practical theology; they are living, creative forms of theology.

Preaching

Beyond one-line proverbs and sayings, some of the speakers stand up and preach a brief sermon that is often based on a Scripture text. They make effective use of repetition, pauses, extended metaphor, and variation in rhythm and volume. The speaker might break eye contact with the group, look up at the ceiling, then look down at the floor, pace in front of the podium, and then return to the audience with a forceful summarizing statement. This performance requires listening responders who play a role in the dramatic event of sermon delivery with their supportive responses. Here is one example, which took a little over thirty seconds to deliver but which contained many features of classical Black Church preaching.

Speaker: I'm going to light this candle today because I'm going to declare and decree for each and every one of us sitting here, we are about to hear some [*long pause, low voice*] good news. Good news.

Group: Good news, Amen, Aaa-men.

Speaker: Good news. Whatever it is, it's always [*pause*] good news.

Individual: Thank you, Jesus.

Speaker: Look at Jeremiah, he said, "I know every thoughts, and I think toward you thoughts of peace and not of evil to give you an expected end."[16] That sounds like some . . .

Individual: Good news.

Speaker: . . . Good news. Come on, y'all; speak it out of your mouth 'cause I got some good news today. So I'm just bringing some good news today. I just feel like that's what we need, to encourage each other.

---

16. This quote departs from the Jeremiah text. The actual text from Jeremiah is "For I know the thoughts that I think toward you, saith the Lord, thoughts of peace, and not of evil, to give you an expected end" (Jer 29:11–12 KJV).

Group: Amen; amen; thank you, Lord; yes, yes; good news; thank you.

He never spoke the content of the good news. It seemed that merely his use of a familiar term, *good news*, and a performance that combined preaching voice, posture, and gesture were enough to invite an energetic response from the group, indicating that we had entered a different space. Long pauses heightened the drama. Skilled use of language and timing initiated a period of call and response that intimated a different world, a sacred world, a world of liminality, "betwixt and between," where anything can happen.[17] Another man brought the following message.[18]

———

Today, I'm finding out that I need to *get in where I fit in*.
   I'm getting in where I fit in because the bottom line is,
   I know who got my back.
   I know who took care of Joseph in the book of Genesis.
   God had his back.
   His brother sold him into slavery.
   But *he got in where he fit in*, and God delivered him.
   He went from the pit to the palace in seventeen years.
   It's a process, sure, and we like our immediate gratification, our microwave living.
   But see, sometimes we got to put those things on the side and trust God.
   Get in where you fit in 'cause God got your back.
   He's got my back. I still owe rent money from last month.
   But I'm not even worried about it.
   God got my back. I trust God. I trust God more today than yesterday.
   . . . So I'm learning today to *get in where you fit in* because God got your back.

———

17. See Victor Turner, *The Ritual Process: Structure and Anti-structure* (New York: Aldine de Gruyter, 1995), 138.
18. I have marked with italics and underlining matching phrases.

Copious use of repetition marked this brief message. Using metaphor, alliteration, Scripture, it was delivered in a recognizable cadence and tone of voice. He spoke slowly so we could let the message take hold.[19] The messages these two men brought were short, but they were able to transform a plain room—lit with fluorescent lights, furnished with folding tables covered with orange plastic tablecloths—into the site of ritual speech and performance familiar to many and no doubt evocative of realms beyond life in a homeless shelter.

Testimony

While *preaching* is bringing a word of encouragement or an exposition of Scripture, *testimony* is witnessing to God acts in the life of the individual. It may be about a mysterious recovery from cancer after someone prayed for them. It may be about resisting the urge to relapse from sobriety with the help of the Lord. It may be about an unexpected gift of money or housing or shoes or a bus ticket or another much-needed requirement for survival. It may be a longer narrative of a life lost to the streets until coming back to God and starting a new life. Sometimes personal testimony is delivered in musical form. A singer will move to the front of the room, compose themselves, and begin to sing an improvised musical testimony of events in their own life. It is clear that the words are personal because they refer to specific events in the person's life, such as homelessness, the shelter, and addiction, and the melody seems to be created in the moment as well.[20] The testimonies are meant to give God the glory and to renew hope in others.

Often, people start their time at the podium with the words "I thank God for waking me up this morning."[21] It may be followed by

---

19. Henry H. Mitchell in *Black Preaching: The Recovery of a Powerful Art* (Nashville: Abingdon, 1990), 88–99, gives a thorough review of the characteristic style and use of language and voice in preaching in Black churches.

20. I have observed this practice in other Black churches as well. See my *Caring Cultures: How Congregations Respond to the Sick* (Waco, TX: Baylor University Press, 2009).

21. This is no doubt taken from some variety of this prayer familiar in many churches: "Thank you, God, for waking me up this morning; for putting shoes on my feet, clothes on my back and food on my table. Thank you, God, for health and strength and the activities of my limbs. Thank you that I woke up this morning clothed in

"in my right mind" or be another form of expression for making it through the night, such as taking another breath, seeing another day, or opening one's eyes and being able to see. I wondered why people would bother to go forward and simply string together phrases with no personal content. I wondered if it was a feeling of obligation or a matter of wanting group affirmation. Maybe it was healing and empowering simply to be seen, beheld, by the saints in the room. It could have been that they wanted to give a nod to participation while avoiding any self-disclosure, thus the rote recitation of a string of familiar sayings and phrases. What I discovered, of course, is that they were performing a ritual form of testimony using time-honored phrases that connected them to God and to the community.

An ethnography of a Black church conducted over thirty-five years ago in a different state describes an almost identical form—the inclusion of "stock phrases in prayers and testimonies" and even thanksgiving for waking up this morning. It described some testimonies that have very little personal content, "no more than the repetition of a set of formulaic phrases, without notable individual variation." Far from being considered unoriginal or uninspired, at the Prayer Service, "the use of certain well-worn phrases invariably brings about an enthusiastic, emotional response, much more than a less formulaic statement with the same content would evoke." The researcher told of a time when he was praying for safety on his upcoming trip. The prayers prayed earlier by others in the group had been met with "heartfelt" response by the group, but he noticed his own prayer evoked no response. Then, in the middle of his prayer, one man in the group prayed over his words, saying, "We ask for your traveling mercies," and the whole group responded, "Yes, Lord."[22] I often have similar experiences, where my careful explicatory words are received without comment, and the well-worn words of someone after me, delivered in a different form and cadence, evokes multiple responses.

One particular day in the Prayer Service, we heard more than one testimony from Cherie.

my right mind." Thomas Hoyt Jr., "Testimony," in *Practicing Our Faith: A Way of Life for a Searching People*, ed. Dorothy C. Bass (San Francisco: Jossey-Bass, 2011), 94.

22. Nelson, *Every Time I Feel*, 164, 110, 165, 51.

When I first met Cherie several months earlier, she was sobbing in big heaves and wailing, "I want to get high! I want to get high! My cousins died; my sister has cancer. . . . I want to get high so bad. I've never wanted it so bad. I want heroin. But I don't want it from around here. I want Jersey or New York heroin." Her words poured out, telling me she was bipolar, she hadn't taken her medicine, she was just out of a psychiatric hospital where she had been for a year, she had been raped there, and on and on her words gushed and wailed forth.

Now, in the Prayer Service, Cherie stood up looking fresh, calm, and happy, and she testified that she would be moving into new housing that very day after several months in the shelter. We celebrated with her.

After Cherie's good news, Rick reported he was still struggling with a gunshot from several years ago. In response, Cherie testified a second time that she had been dead for fourteen minutes after using heroin laced with fentanyl and then was brought back to life. She had prayed to live, and God brought her back to life. We all gave thanks again.

Then a man stood up and told us he had been diagnosed with bipolar disorder, schizophrenia, depression, and other mental illnesses. We never knew where his story was heading because Cherie burst forth for the third time, saying, "I am *extremely* mentally ill! Just ask Chaplain! I'm bipolar, and I was bouncing off the walls when I got here. Now I'm moving into my own place!"

I did not even attempt to respond to the pain of the man who had been shot or to the man with multiple mental health problems. It was Cherie who had the experience and the authority to respond. First, she confirmed God's power to preserve life in the face of death, whether by bullet or toxic drugs, and then she burst forth with her announcement of her deep mental illness, all for the building up of another's hope and humanity. It was as though she were saying, "Look at me; through all my trials and brokenness, I am now moving on to a new life. And God will do the same for you." The heart of her testimony and her authority to testify were a combination of an extraordinary divine healing after fourteen minutes of death and her emphatic assertion of her stigmatized life and illness. Her declaration reminded me of Paul's assertion of his apostolic authority based on his greater suffering: "far greater labors, far more imprisonments, with countless floggings, and often near death" (2 Cor 11:23).

The paucity of my experience with the forms of suffering displayed in the Prayer Service limited my empathic efficacy. My lack of experience with religious forms such as testimony limited my ability to offer hope or encouragement. But I did have relationships with Cherie and Rick, and I brought them together in the Prayer Service, and they could minister to each other. The capacity for Cherie to connect with their pain and to bring hope hints at an affirmation of Jesus's death and resurrection. She was a living example of someone who endured wounds of the mind and flesh just as they had, and she stood as an embodied proclamation of resurrection into a new life.

Another time during a discussion after the Prayer Service, Joy told a story that took the form of testimony.

———

Once, I was in the pouring rain, and I didn't know where gas would come from. Weakness showed up: I could just pop some pills and call it a day. I popped two. Tears were rolling down my face. Lo and behold, a man came, and twenty dollars just flew out of this man's hand. There was a folded twenty-dollar bill on the ground. It was a miraculous thing God had done.

———

Without a pause, she went immediately into a second story of God's blessings.

———

I came early to get a bed on the bottom bunk. I tried to park on the lot. A not-too-hospitable person said cops might come, but you can take a chance. I said, "God, I'm going to put this in your hands." I [my car] was not disturbed.

———

People in the Prayer Service who heard Joy's testimonies offered two accounts of their significance. The first was "You hear another's testimony and it *builds your faith*. God desires us to strengthen each other" (emphasis mine). In other words, this account was deemed a vehicle for "strengthening" others. The second interpretation of this testimony was that it was a witness that "*miracles happen*"; God still acts in this "mean old world" (emphasis mine).[23]

―――――

These are not coincidences! That money that was dropped was predestiny. Miracles happen. I thank God because I need it. It helps me treat people the way I would like to be treated. It's a mean old world almost unfit to live in. We must separate ourselves from the world and let God do his business.

―――――

The testimonies are not delivered only as a recitation of facts but are offered for communal purposes, and the community members, in turn, add their interpretations of them. The entire event is a communal one, involving speaker and hearer who, in turn, becomes a speaker.[24]

Music

The introduction of a song is an embodied, sensual form of theologizing. People move, close their eyes, and hum or sing or clap. The Prayer Service does not include a specific time for group singing, but in almost every gathering, someone makes a spontaneous musical offering. They are usually from a repertoire of music from

―――――――――

23. James Cone writes of testimony as offering both individual and communal edification. He says, "Testimony is a spiritually liberating experience wherein he/she is empowered by God's Holy Spirit to stay on the 'gospel train' until it reaches the kingdom. Although testimony is unquestionably personal and thus primarily an individual's story, it is also a story accessible to others in the community of faith. Indeed, the purpose of testimony is not only to strengthen an individual's faith but also to build the faith of the community." James Cone, *My Soul Looks Back* (Nashville: Abingdon, 1982), 11–12, quoted in Lee Butler, "Testimony as Hope and Care," in *Living Stones in the Household of God*, ed. Linda Elaine Thomas (Minneapolis: Augsburg Fortress, 2004), 25.

24. See Hoyt, "Testimony," 89–102. Hoyt places testimony in the history of the Black Church.

a former time. Some will smile and say, "I have not heard that in a *long* time."

> Without him, I can do nothing.
> Without him, I surely will fail.
> Without him, I can do nothing.
> Just like a ship without a sail.[25]

Or,

> Hold to his hand, to God's unchanging hand.
> Hold to his hand, God's unchanging hand.
> You got to build your life on things eternal.
> You got to hold to God's unchanging hand.[26]

Or,

> If you live right, heaven belongs to you.
> If you live right, heaven belongs to you.
> If you live right, heaven belongs to you.
> Heaven belongs to you.[27]

The songs are usually out of my repertoire, but there are some very familiar songs that are offered.

> He's got the whole world in his hands . . .
> Will the circle be unbroken . . .
> This little light of mine . . .

---

25. Mylon Le Fevre, "Without Him I Could Do Nothing," in *African American Heritage Hymnal*, ed. Rev. Dr. Delores Carpenter and Rev. Nolan E. Williams Jr. (Chicago: GIA, 2001), hymn 515.

26. Jennie Wilson, "Hold to God's Unchanging Hand," in *African American Heritage Hymnal*, ed. Rev. Dr. Delores Carpenter and Rev. Nolan E. Williams Jr. (Chicago: GIA, 2001), hymn 404.

27. Jimmie Abingdon, arr., "If You Live Right, Heaven Belongs to You," in *African American Heritage Hymnal*, hymn 582.

However, when I have initiated hymns that are considered classics in my tradition, such as "Holy, Holy, Holy," "What a Friend We Have in Jesus," and "Fairest Lord Jesus," many do sing along. Their church music repertoire is not limited to gospel music.

Often, at the end of the service, I will play a recorded piece of music and say that the music is for prayer and reflection. Almost always, over years' time, every single person in the room is making some sort of bodily response. There may be hands raised in the air with eyes closed, full-blown singing along, heads or torsos swaying back and forth, hands patting the table or a lap, heads shaking back and forth, hands seeming to grasp something invisible in the air, hands clapping, or lightly tapping feet. Music evokes an almost universal corporeal response in the Prayer Service; it creates a "prayerful, excited, connective set of bodily gestures, dispositions, and actions."[28] Describing her reaction to dimming lights in worship in preparation for a baptism, one theologian describes her "body knowing instinctively not only when to lean forward in my seat but also how to open myself to something I would describe as sacred once I'm in the lean."[29] The link between deep knowing, bodily movement, and the sacred is evident as music is played in the Prayer Service. At the risk of overstating the effect of music in our Prayer Service, I wonder if this is an occasion where the "black body is rescued temporarily from the physical ramifications of poverty in that the body becomes a vessel for cosmic energy." Music can decenter the deprivations and humiliations of poverty, including their effects on the body. Anthony Pinn says, "The physical consequences of poverty felt through the body are of limited effect when God has manifested God's power, beauty, and purpose through black bodies."[30] I would add, the physical consequences of living without a home are mitigated when God's power, beauty, and purpose are manifest through Black bodies moving in response to pieces of music in the Prayer Service.[31]

---

28. Natalie Wigg-Stevenson, *Ethnographic Theology: An Inquiry into the Production of Theological Knowledge* (New York: Palgrave Macmillan, 2014), 51.

29. Wigg-Stevenson, 51.

30. Pinn, "Warm Bodies, Cold Currency," 240, 241.

31. See Jon Michael Spencer, *Protest and Praise: Sacred Music of Black Religion* (Nashville: Fortress, 1990).

ORALITY AND LITERACY
IN THE PRAYER SERVICE

Part of what accounts for the differences between my communication style and others' style may be the difference between orality and literacy. In a purely oral culture, "there are no texts," and "you know what you recall." Thus rhythm, repetition, and patterns are important for retaining knowledge and wisdom within an oral culture. Words not captured in a written text are fleeting; they exist only for the moment that they are spoken, for the duration of the time that the sound of them lingers in the air. The "evanescent world of sound" means that spoken words are ephemeral *events* as opposed to solidified *things* that are retained in written form.[32] The importance of pattern and the event-like character of words help explain the difference between my explanatory prose and the patterned event of the spoken words of people who come to the Prayer Service. Even the written documents by Missionary Richey had the character of sound event in them.

My words, on the other hand, were the result of twelve years of primary and secondary school and twelve more years of undergraduate and graduate school, during which precise, logically sequenced written expression was highly prized. However, "writing fosters abstractions" that are removed from where people live, love, hate, struggle, and die. Furthermore, "writing separates the knower from the known and thus sets up conditions for 'objectivity' in the sense of personal disengagement or distancing."[33] The Scripture, sayings, and wordplay offered in the Prayer Service have an immediacy and relationality to them that my efforts to clearly communicate concepts did not have.[34] My words were connections to ideas; their words were connections to each other through the invocation of a

---

32. Walter Ong, *Orality and Literacy: The Technologizing of the Word* (New York: Routledge, 2002), 33, 90.
33. Ong, 43, 45.
34. See Tex Sample, *Ministry in an Oral Culture: Living with Will Rogers, Uncle Remus, and Minnie Pearl* (Louisville, KY: Westminster John Knox, 1994). Tex Sample describes the encounter between students trained in clinical pastoral education and whom he calls "hard-living people." After hearing about a difficult experience, students would ask the introspective question, "How did that make you feel?" In response, rather than the disclosure of internal dispositions, they were told a story.

shared archive of sayings or, in the case of Missionary Richey's novel sayings, shared forms.

It must be emphasized here that to have skills in an oral culture is not at all to say that one does not also have facility in the literary, intellectual skills of reasoning and abstract thinking or the cognitive capacities to read and write complex thought. Rather, it is to say that being steeped in an oral culture opens ways of communicating and connecting that are beyond mere prose explication.

If my efforts to bring a pastoral word to the Prayer Service are motivated by a desire to painstakingly find the words to explain how and in what form God is here in spite of all evidence to the contrary, "the language of the oral tradition [in the Prayer Service] is held to *suggest* meaning without explicitly stating information." The truth of a saying is "verified by the experience of listeners."[35] Thus oral tradition's power in the Prayer Service is in the way the skilled speaker is able to find a fitting saying for the situation that resonates with the hearers' experience, not in the speaker's explication of content independent of the experience of the hearers.

Shelter Practical Theology

The right fit is an aspect of in situ practical theologizing. The testimonies and brief sermons and insights are regularly applied to particular circumstances of pain, discouragement, and disappointment. The people uttering them are active, in the moment, practical theologians. Some are particularly skillful in matching the right proverb for a particular situation. For example, if a woman is telling us about the strong temptation to return to life on the streets, someone in the service might say with conviction, "The devil is *real.*" Everyone would nod in agreement and offer supportive phrases, and it would be clear that the saying matched the situation. This exchange represents a communal form of practical theology unfolding in the Prayer Service where a skilled theological thinker was able to bring together a lived situation with a fitting saying, and it is affirmed

---

35. Shirley Brice Heath, "Protean Shapes in Literacy Events: Ever-Shifting Oral and Literate Traditions," in *Spoken and Written Language: Advances in Discourse Processes*, ed. Deborah Tannen (Norwood, NJ: Ablex, 1982), 91 (emphasis mine).

by the group. The practical theologian of the moment brought the situation of temptation into the cosmic drama of the battle between God's faithful and the devil, joining her to the faithful of all generations and placing her story in the context of a world controlled by a transcendent and powerful God. Then this practical theological utterance was endorsed by the vocal response of the worshippers.[36] This coalescence of content, genre, fit, and communal endorsement can be understood as the production of practical theology. According to Bonnie Miller-McLemore, "At its most basic level, practical theology is performed by those who thoughtfully seek to embody deep convictions about life and its ultimate meaning in the midst of ordinary and extraordinary circumstances."[37] In this sense, the participants of the Prayer Service are performing practical theology in their skilled deployment of core religious beliefs/sayings.

One such "extraordinary circumstance" was the death of popular singer Whitney Houston. Deaths in the sphere of popular culture are noted with particular attention in the Prayer Service. For example, the deaths of Michael Jackson and Don Cornelius were discussed frequently. One woman held her head in her hands and mourned the loss of "our Michael." They did not receive as much attention as the death of Ms. Houston, however. Her death received even more discussion and prayerful attention than the more recent events surrounding the deaths of Trayvon Martin, Michael Brown, and Sandra Bland. After Whitney Houston's death, the practical theologizing began immediately as people sought to affirm the power and presence of God in the midst of tragic death. Several people expressed confidence that she was saved. One woman said that God took her so that the devil couldn't have her. Another woman said that God wanted to show everyone how bad drug use is. Still

---

36. Practical theologian Dale P. Andrews coined the term *hearer response* to describe the "reader response process and oral culture" in *Practical Theology for Black Churches*, 125.

37. Bonnie Miller-McLemore, "Practical Theology," in *Encyclopedia of Religion in America*, ed. Charles H. Lippy and Peter Williams (Washington, DC: CQ, 2010), 1741. Elsewhere, Miller-McLemore articulates four understandings of practical theology: "It is a *discipline* among scholars and an *activity of faith* among believers . . . [and] a *method* for studying theology in practice and it is a *curricular area* of subdisciplines in the seminary." Miller-McLemore, "The Contributions of Practical Theology," in *The Wiley-Blackwell Companion to Practical Theology*, ed. Bonnie Miller-McLemore (Malden, MA: Wiley-Blackwell, 2012), 5.

another woman said that it was God's way of saying he wanted us to all be closer to each other. The larger theological belief deployed here is that "all things work together for good to them that love God" (Rom 8:28 KJV). It is a profound affirmation of the Providence of God and God's omnipotent power, which is above all and through all. Nothing falls outside God's power in the world and God's plan for it.[38] One of the findings of recent qualitative research on Black grief was displayed in the service: there is widespread belief that God had good reasons for taking the one who died.[39] Practical theological reflection was an immediate response to the event of her death.

Another death was in the local news. Gunshots were fired inside a house the night before, and two young men were killed. The day after this event, a woman went to the podium in the Prayer Service and told us that one of the young men who were killed was her daughter's boyfriend. Then she told us about her church experience on the morning before the shooting. Normally, she does not shout in church, she said, but this Sunday, she had a feeling "all throughout her body" that she should shout, and she did so throughout the service. If she had not praised God in that way, she said, her daughter would have gone to the house with her boyfriend. She concluded that it was her shouting that saved her daughter, saying, "When the praise goes up, the blessings come down." For her, her body was the vehicle of her message to God, and the movements of her body in extended shout were the faithful act that invoked God's blessing in the form of protection for her daughter. In an act of practical theologizing, the belief that God will bless the faithful combined with a familiar saying stood at the core of her practical theologizing about an event in her personal life and our shared civic life.

The Distinctiveness of the Prayer Service

My earliest thoughts on the prayers and testimonies in the Prayer Service romanticized the faith of the poor who trusted a God who

---

38. See the discussion of Providence in Nicholas Cooper-Lewter and Henry H. Mitchell, *Soul Theology: The Heart of American Black Culture* (Nashville: HarperCollins, 1986), 14–28.

39. Paul C. Rosenblatt and Beverly R. Wallace, *African American Grief* (New York: Routledge, 2005), 111.

will save them, whose profound theological insights emerged out of their individual experiences of the fires of suffering and deliverance. Later, I realized that their theological beliefs did not spring full blown from their proximity to God and their extraordinary individual piety but from the religio-cultural soup in which they developed: mostly a Black version of southern Evangelicalism. Most beliefs, ritual practices, and forms of piety are indeed recognizable as coming from that source. Yet the Prayer Service is distinctive as a place where all faith traditions are honored; it is not labeled as a specifically Christian space. From the very beginning, our publicity has included the following statement: "Everyone is welcome at this service. Whether you are Baptist, Pentecostal, Methodist, Catholic, Jewish, Muslim, Hindu, Buddhist, or from another tradition or from no tradition at all, or have not decided yet, *you are invited*."

This message has been appropriated by Prayer Service regulars, who repeat the statement to newcomers. There is no pressure to adopt a particular belief in order to be accepted. In a focus group, one man said,

———

This is a place we can all lay our swords down. We come with different backgrounds, different problems, but we can resonate together, get on the same wavelength. We have all had different failures, but we can all share a common victory.

———

Baptist, Methodist, nondenominational, and Pentecostal traditions have been represented, and there has been a regular attender who used Hindu prayer style, a few from Muslim traditions, at least one goddess worshipper, Catholics who cross themselves, and a very few people who speak of doubting God's existence. They are all met with welcome and encouragement. If there is anything novel about the Prayer Service, it is the consistent adherence to inclusivity.

The inclusivity also extends to grace offered to people who have committed terrible acts. This was powerfully displayed regarding one of our participants.

One day in the Prayer Service, someone announced that Malcolm had been arrested again. He was tall, slender, and in his sixties, and I often heard him joking with others as he stood in line for lunch. I knew he lived with chronic pain and participated in a dual diagnosis (substance abuse and mental illness) program, but his presence at the shelter exuded style, suavity. Over time, I learned that he had served a nineteen-year sentence for second-degree murder. It was said that he killed his father when he found him in bed with Malcolm's wife. Actually, he killed his father in 1985, but he had already accidentally killed his wife in 1980. It is also said that his father's murder was accompanied by extreme brutality. I read in the newspaper archives that he cut his father's head off.[40] When he came to the Prayer Service, the only song he ever sang was "None but the Righteous Shall See God." Was this his theological interpretation of his life and future? Did he live with terror over his eternal soul? He lived with pain in his body and surely pain in his soul. No doubt both contributed to his ongoing drinking.

I heard he had been arrested, so I looked online for more information and found a newspaper report that he had been arrested for stealing from a Dollar General store. During that search, I stumbled onto a website that substituted its own headline for the same newspaper article: "3 Felonious C[——]ns Arrested in Dollah Genrul Armed Robbery" (deletion mine), followed by still more hideous racist comments.[41] To understand Malcolm, his life, his struggles, his pain, and his missteps, one would have to include the context of vicious racism into which he was born. Malcolm's crimes could have been linked to his mental illness and addiction, but the context of brutal racism certainly played a role in the course of his life. In order to respond pastorally to Malcolm, in order to draw near to the places of pain and suffering, shame and guilt, the wounds and broken places, one would have to see him in the context of a ravaging, dehumanizing racism.

We had not seen Malcolm for a while at the Prayer Service. Then we learned that he had died. Missionary Richey and I went to the funeral. Back at the Prayer Service at UMD, there was a great deal of affirmation that no matter what anyone said, God had forgiven him and that he was in heaven, and it is time to let the past

---

40. *Hendersonville Times-News*, April 30, 1985, 16.
41. Due to the deeply offensive nature of this website, the citation is intentionally omitted.

go and not hold it against him. This remembrance of people who have passed through, and this sustained loyalty to them beyond their death and in spite of their sins, characterizes the Prayer Service at its best.

Prayer Service as Unscripted Space

What is significant about the sayings, testimonies, and sermons that appear in the Prayer Service is that they are generated by the participants themselves. There are no overt ritual templates, no theological litmus tests, no doctrinal standards. It is an unscripted space for the performance of people's religious expression. The style of the service goes through seasons depending on who is attending from among the people who pass through the shelter. At times, it will be more focused on the works of the devil, other times on a Mosaic work's righteousness. Sometimes there are more singers and fewer preachers; other times there are people who often share a Scripture text or a reading from a devotional booklet. What abides is the simple formula "light a candle, say a prayer." This blank slate allows the researcher to see what phrases, sayings, songs (recorded and sung), bodily comportment, rhetorical forms, and audience responses emerge in the midst of a difficult, fluid, and often chaotic time in people's lives.

If participation in the Prayer Service surfaces various *forms* of religious expression, one-on-one conversations allow the researcher to focus on the content of people's *beliefs*, how people interpret their lives of pain, joy, dejection, and faith in their own religious idiom.

CHAPTER 3

LIVING BELIEFS

Many people who arrive at the shelter to eat or sleep bring with them religious beliefs and practices.[1] Under conditions of dislocation or deprivation, something of religion has endured. Even while disconnected from people and communities where they first absorbed an understanding of the divine and religious practice, people who come to Urban Ministries of Durham (UMD) continue to call upon God's name and engage in behaviors considered religious. They come to the shelter with a "repertoire of capacities" that endures in spite of conditions of living without a home or adequate food.[2]

Belief can mean a propositional statement that is codified in doctrine or creed and to which one assents. When I was the pastor of a small church, from time to time, a visitor would say to me, "I like this church. What do you have to believe to become a member?"

---

1. R. Stephen Warner describes immigrants who come to the United States and "bring their religions with them, and gathering religiously is one of the ways they make a life here. Their religious identities often (but not always) mean more to them away from home, in their diaspora, than they did before." R. Stephen Warner, introduction to *Gatherings in Diaspora: Religious Communities and the New Migration*, ed. R. Stephen Warner and Judith G. Wittner (Philadelphia: Temple University Press, 1998), 3. One way to understand those who stay at Urban Ministries of Durham (UMD) is that they are a people in exile, cut off from home, origins, and people who and places that made them.

2. I am indebted to Susan Crawford Sullivan for this phrase from Ann Swidler's *Talk of Love: How Culture Matters* (Chicago: University of Chicago Press, 2001), 81. Sullivan, *Living Faith: Everyday Religion and Mothers in Poverty* (Chicago: University of Chicago Press, 2011), 50.

I imagined this visitor assumed that assenting to the truth of certain orthodox statements was the gateway to membership, statements such as "Jesus died for my sins" or "God created the world in seven days." However, my small congregation, like many other mainline Protestant churches, embodied something akin to a "Golden Rule Christianity" where there is a "different orthodoxy," one less defined by adherence to particular doctrines and more defined by particular practices and ways of living.[3] We were not as interested in particular "cognitive or ideological structures" but very concerned about practices such as caring "for relationships, doing good deeds, and looking for opportunities to provide care and comfort for people in need."[4]

Religious belief involves much more than teachings, doctrines, or creeds. A text-based or propositionally based definition of religious belief omits much of what is at the heart of a religious life. It does not include *intersubjective* experiences of love, care, support, or possibly rejection, manipulation, or abuse. It also ignores the ways *bodies* are implicated in religion. The movements of the body—kneeling, swaying, clapping, and embrace—are left out, as well as the body's constriction or discipline. Nor does it include the *senses*, such as the "official" smell of incense and the unintentional smells of the moldy basement and fish frying. The experience of the religious life also includes the tactile, such as the feel of the wooden pew and the thin, crispy pages of the Bible. There are "official" elements of the visual, such as the cross, an icon, and pulpit paraments, as well as the font of the hymnal, old maps of the Holy Land, and dusty silk flowers on the bookshelf. Sounds include songs, hymns, and anthems, as well as the creaking wooden floor and the screech of the microphone feedback. The ways *architecture* divides, encloses, discloses, unifies, channels the gaze, and modifies sound are spatial ways of experiencing the religious. Along with textual elements, religious beliefs are saturated with the intersubjective, embodied, sensual, and spatial.

---

3. Nancy T. Ammerman, "Golden Rule Christianity: Lived Religion in the American Mainstream," in *Lived Religion in America: Toward a History of Practice*, ed. David D. Hall (Princeton, NJ: Princeton University Press, 1997), 201.

4. Ammerman, 201–2.

For example, to assert the belief that "God will provide" carries with it the relationship or community in which it was taught and sustained. It carries memories of bodies cared for in infirmity and alive in acts of praise. Intrinsic to it are visual images of the face of a living person or a picture in the church basement. For many, to access the deepest place of belief in God's faithfulness requires strains of music heard or sung.

Furthermore, the realm of belief cannot be confined to official religious sites. Much of the practice of religion is in the context of the home. Around the kitchen table, overhearing the adults, listening to the car radio, prayers at meals and bedtime, and Scripture and sayings uttered for advice, warning, comfort, and explanation are key sources of religious beliefs and practices. These intersubjective, bodily, and textual elements in the domestic sphere also create religious worlds. Thus when I speak of the religion of people at UMD, I do not mean just a bucket of propositional statements that are declared true by believers. Rather, I mean the religious worlds they occupy, their belief worlds or belief landscapes.[5] These belief landscapes are where people live, choose, respond, hope, despair, love, sacrifice, and serve, which are absorbed through the intersubjective, the bodily, as well as through the cognitive.

However, I cannot describe enduring webs of relationships or a developed material culture of the people at the shelter.[6] The particular characteristics of the people I am studying mean that certain realms of inquiry are limited. This study of the religion of people without homes, with few possessions, and with limited affiliations sets it apart from other well-known ethnographies of religious worlds. The variety of practices and material culture of women in eastern North Carolina, as well as the material culture and resources of people following the prosperity gospel in Jamaica, have been

---

5. Serene Jones, *Feminist Theory and Christian Theology: Cartographies of Grace* (Minneapolis: Augsburg Fortress, 2000), 17.
6. Cynthia Ann Curtis is one theological ethnographer who was able to describe three social worlds of people without homes in Nashville, TN. Curtis, "Spiritualities of the Displaced: An Ethnographic Study of Homeless Lived Faith" (PhD diss., Duke University School of Divinity, 2013).

beautifully described.[7] Discussions of religion have moved beyond the realm of belief to include the body and its adornments, giving attention to "how and what people eat, how they dress, how they deal with birth and death and sexuality and nature, even how they modify hair and body through tattoos or dreadlocks."[8] The evolution of a community and how it variously responded to race is the subject of another study.[9] One study of Evangelical women describes the decor of monthly meeting spaces, contents of publications, and events at a particular winter retreat.[10] However, people without any material resources or enduring dwelling places are very limited in their choices in these matters, and thus the researcher's access to enduring cultural traits is more limited. When one has no home, when one owns nothing, literally, but the clothes on their back, religious material culture is limited, and when one is removed from home, one's personal space, relational webs, and religious ties are spare. The transience, the material scarcity, and fragile relational webs make this study different from other recent ethnographies of religious worlds.

For example, the possessions of people staying at UMD may be a reflection of what was available in the clothing closet more than a link to a coherent culture. I eventually learned not to offer comments—such as "I've been to that beach" or "That's a good restaurant/church/hotel. When were you there?"—on what was printed on a T-shirt. It gave rise to awkward responses because their shirts reflected the shelter clothing closet, not their experiences. Similarly, the possessions carried by people I meet may be what were left after they were robbed while sleeping in a parking garage,

---

7. Marla Frederick, *Between Sundays: Black Women and Everyday Struggles of Faith* (Berkeley: University of California Press, 2003); Frederick, *Colored Television: American Religion Gone Global* (Stanford, CA: Stanford University Press, 2016).

8. Nancy T. Ammerman, "Finding Religion in Everyday Life," *Sociology of Religion* 75, no. 2 (June 2014): 190. According to Ammerman, "Lived religion may include the spaces people inhabit, as well—the construction of shrines in homes or in public places, for instance. And it includes the physical and artistic things people do together, such as singing, dancing, and other folk or community traditions that enact a spiritual sense of solidarity and transcendence" (190–91).

9. Mary McClintock Fulkerson, *Places of Redemption: Theology for a Worldly Church* (New York: Oxford University Press, 2007).

10. R. Marie Griffith, *God's Daughters: Evangelical Women and the Power of Submission* (Berkeley: University of California Press, 1997).

not an accurate depiction of their cultural origins. They have limited power over choices within the realm of materiality. In addition, relational contexts are often thin, fragile, and fleeting; they experience "the poverty of tenuous connections."[11] The connections with family and the faith community are often fragmented and may be fraught with disappointments, betrayals, and traumatic memories. The relational ruptures may have originated in family-based abuse, or it could be that the unsheltered person lives with a substance use disorder or a serious mental illness that has fractured relationships. Churches are inconsistent in their acceptance of unsheltered people, and thus religious affiliation is fraught with obstacles. Lack of social connections may also be the result of an attempt to start a new life in a new city. When affiliations with church, a faith group, and family are rare, it is hard to describe the social context of their religious practices. Ecclesial practices endure and are reproduced to a degree in the Prayer Service, but they appear as shards of a tradition that are displaced from the context in which they emerged. They are practices in exile.[12]

Thus I have looked at what can be studied: the *forms* and *beliefs* that they bring to the Prayer Service and that are revealed in the stories of God's presence in their lives, practices of personal piety in the form of prayer and Bible reading, invocations of

---

11. Pamela Couture, *Seeing Children, Seeing God: A Practical Theology of Children* (Nashville: Abingdon, 2000), 14, quoted in Jill Snodgrass, "Shelters or Sanctuaries: Practical Theology, Pastoral Care and Counseling, and Homelessness" (PhD diss., Claremont School of Theology, 2010), 229. What Couture says about the spare relationships of children in poverty can also be said of adults living without homes.

12. When reading ethnographic and sociological studies of other sites, the distinctiveness of studying religion in a homeless shelter becomes clear. Studies of lived religion and the material culture of religion contain descriptions of religious worlds that involve architectural context, particular foods, bodily ritual, characteristic comportment, clothing, and many more rich and varied elements. See Hall, *Lived Religion in America*; and David Morgan, *Religion and Material Culture: The Matter of Belief* (New York: Routledge, 2010). Nancy Ammerman refers to "the peculiar Protestant lineage of our sociological preoccupation with belief," recognizing the limits of focusing on belief alone for the study of religion. Ammerman, "Finding Religion in Everyday Life," 190. However, this study does rely heavily on statements of belief because ownership of material goods and membership in communal entities, and habits of visiting particular sites of religious observance, are severely limited.

sayings and Scripture texts, and habits of narrating their lives in a religious idiom. The very fact of the endurance of these pieces of religious life is what makes them worthy of study. I press the question of why these elements endured and conclude they endured because they enable survival in harsh circumstances.

Having emerged in the context of suffering—primarily the suffering wrought by violent, subjugating racism and its material consequence, deep poverty—these beliefs enable survival in the midst of harsh circumstances, and they function as a form of resistance to powers that would dehumanize them and deprive them of the means to survive and thrive. Together, these beliefs are not supposed to be "logically coherent"; rather, they have a "practical coherence."[13] To have practical coherence, "it needs to make sense in one's everyday life, and it needs to be effective, to 'work,' in the sense of accomplishing some desired end (such as healing, improving one's relationship with a loved one, or harvesting enough food to last the winter)."[14] There are multiple "desired ends" accomplished by the beliefs I hear at the shelter. One such end is the fact that they serve as a basis of connecting to other people who share them, and uttering them in a communal context offers a sense of belonging. Another desirable end is the affirmation of one's worthiness to receive help and to have a better life. They give hope and offer peace and patience, and they generate energy, fuel, to persist in all that must be done to secure shelter or to endure life without shelter. Culled largely from Black forms of religion, they "push against the dehumanizing consequences of poverty."[15]

For the majority of people at the shelter, these deep archives of beliefs had their origins in the context of what Blacks have endured for centuries: slavery, Jim Crow, lynchings, deep poverty, and other forms of focused, violent racism.[16] The wounds wrought

---

13. Meredith McGuire, *Lived Religion: Faith and Practice in Everyday Life* (New York: Oxford University Press, 2008), 15.

14. McGuire, 15.

15. Pinn, "Warm Bodies, Cold Currency," 228.

16. See Jason E. Shelton and Michael O. Emerson, *Blacks and Whites in Christian America: How Racial Discrimination Shapes Religious Convictions* (New York: New York University Press, 2012). Shelton and Emerson also highlight the context in which Black religion emerged as well as its function in the present: "African Americans remain committed to a unique form of Protestantism that was born out

by these historical atrocities are the sites of the birth of the theology they bring.[17] It is in the ruptures generated by racism that the core archive of their theologies takes shape.[18] The wounds carried by individuals at the shelter are staggering, and they have inherited theological, ritual, and ecclesial traditions that have been forged in response to these wounds.

The historical wound of violent racism is the larger context of their theology, and local theologies are born in response to the world people inhabit in and around the shelter. Calling upon inherited traditions, theology survives at the wound of present-day deep poverty and living without shelter. In their season of dislocation, the people I meet at UMD pull sustaining beliefs and behaviors from their memories. Bodily postures and comportment as well as phrases, lyrics, and biblical texts are called forth in service of survival. The habits of response to the trials, humiliations, deprivations that life brings remain even under very difficult circumstances.

In order to protect the identities of the people I have interviewed, in most instances, I have disconnected life experiences from theological statements. The problem with this approach is that it makes it difficult to discern the precise function of the theological language they present if their life circumstances are absent from this

---

of—and continues to protect them against—the historical consequences of racial stratification in the United States. . . . African Americans tend to lean on their faith as a supernatural call for help to protect against the consequences of historical and contemporary racial discrimination." Shelton and Emerson, 4.

17. Mary McClintock Fulkerson has written eloquently about theology beginning at the "scene of a wound." She says, "Wounds generate new thinking. Disjunctions birth invention—from a disjuncture in logic, where reason is compelled to find new connections in thought, to brokenness in existence where creativity is compelled to search for possibilities of reconciliation. Like a wound, theological thinking is generated by a sometimes inchoate sense that something *must* be addressed." Fulkerson, *Places of Redemption*, 13. She refers to the work of Walter Lowe, *Theology and Difference: The Wound of Reason* (Bloomington: Indiana University Press, 1993), 9–10.

18. Robert Orsi refers to the interest of scholars of lived religion in the wounded, broken places. He says, "The study of lived religion focuses most on places where people are wounded or broken, because it is in these broken places that religious media become most exigent. It is in such hot cultural moments—at the edges of life, in times of social upheaval, confusion, or transition, when old orders give way and what is ahead remains unclear—that we see what matters most in a religious world." Orsi, "Is the Study of Lived Religion Irrelevant to the World We Live In?," *Journal of the Scientific Study of Religion* 42, no. 2 (2003): 173.

report. The precise meaning, as well as the way a statement functions to fund hope, survival, perseverance, or any other positive orientation, becomes murkier and less precise. In order to mitigate but not erase that fuzziness, I describe here some of the life conditions and personal characteristics of the people whose words appear below.

Almost all are parents. Some sing regularly at the Prayer Service; some display wide knowledge of Scripture. The gifts of kindness, wisdom, gratitude, self-sacrifice, and humor are represented. Some have displayed rage, some have offered tears, and some have engaged in deep laughter. Some have fond memories of their childhood; others can tell stories of neglect and abuse. Many grew up participating in a church. Their ages range from mid-thirties to mid-sixties. Most are Black. Their dwelling places include living at UMD, outside, in family shelters, or in subsidized apartments. Most are sober, several are in recovery from a substance use disorder that lasted from a few years to several decades, and at least one continues in active addiction. Several have served prison or jail sentences that range from short term to over a decade. Jobs include work at a large retail store, clerical work, and the skilled trades. Mental illness, that I am aware of, includes depression and post-traumatic stress disorder (PTSD). Violence has touched them in a variety of ways: a shooting in the head, a shooting in the leg, domestic violence, and a child murdered through a shooting. Income may be from a disability check or a job, but a large portion of them have no income at all. Again, the risk of giving this conglomeration of traits, skills, demographic location, and income is that the meaning and function of biblical and theological language in particular lives in particular situations are less clear. My purpose for offering this list of features of the people whose words appear below is to establish both the difficulty of their lives and their skills, virtues, and resources while respecting their privacy.

God Will Provide

By far, the most frequent references to God are in the context of deep gratitude for providing what we need. God faithfully comes through in times of trouble. "I think about when I have been really, really in some kind of way, it seems like there is no way out; God always send me somebody." Similar to Julian of Norwich, there is a deep sense that "all shall be well." "It's going to be all right. You got to have faith in God. I tell people that all the time now. God will do it. God will take care of it." God is the one who will fulfill our needs, if we have faith. "You got to have faith and God will give you what you need. If you ask for what you need, he will give you what you need." People affirm God's reliability even though they don't see exactly how it will work out.

Dr. Travis Albritton, a professor at the University of Chapel Hill who grew up in a Black Church in rural eastern North Carolina, where "racism is very, very prevalent," often heard the affirmation that God will provide. He says, "It comes out of a sense that God will take care of us in a world that treats us harshly, where we don't have a lot, where we are second class citizens. God will bring us out. God is my provider. . . . You got to trust God, because God is going to work this out for you. God's going to make a way. Can't tell you how, but you hold on, you believe."[19] In a racist context, which threatens, restricts, and controls the lives of Black people, there is a deep confidence in the God whose power is greater than any other.

Turning a problem over to God could be seen as an abdication of responsibility for one's life, as though a person is saying, "I give up. I can't deal with this anymore. God will have to fix this." However, this turn to God who will provide is far from a form of resignation. Rather, "taking a problem in life to God is seen as an *active* step toward its resolution." Thus "faith becomes a tool of resistance, rejecting limits and dehumanization. . . . Believing is an *activity* that taps power." To claim the presence and power of God in a difficult situation "is both a statement of faith and a battle cry."[20]

Often, but not always, the declaration that "God will provide" is accompanied by "if you have faith or if you pray." It is not clear to me whether this is an exchange—as it is in Pentecostal "prevailing prayer," where God is obligated to fulfill your request—or if this is simply a call to sustain a deep trust in God.[21] Having faith or

19. Travis Albritton, face-to-face personal communication, March 20, 2018.
20. Stephanie Mitchem, "Jesus Is My Doctor: Healing and Religion in African American Women's Lives," in *Religion and Healing in America*, ed. Linda Barnes and Susan Starr Sered (New York: Oxford University Press, 2005), 287 (emphasis mine).
21. Grant Wacker, *Heaven Below: Early Pentecostals and American Culture* (Cambridge, MA: Harvard University Press, 2003), 26.

praying may be what to do in the meantime, during the interim, while waiting for an answer to prayer. It could be that it describes an orientation of equanimity, of quiet confidence, of waiting, of peace, of knowing that the situation is in the hands of God. In lives full of stress, to *cast your cares upon the Lord* is a way to release the burden of worry.[22]

Whenever something good happens, God did it. A man reported that he was just hired for a job he wanted. His first words were "God is good." When an unexpected gift would appear, one woman often said, "Look at God!" I have been surprised by the attribution of credit to God at the expense of recognition of human agency. One woman told of being released from a hospital emergency department at three in the morning and not being allowed to stay in the waiting room until bus service resumed in the morning. She went out to the road in the dark and began to walk back to the shelter. Another shelter resident drove up to the hospital to begin his shift. He picked her up, drove right back to the shelter, then came back to work at the hospital. She, as well as the other Prayer Service attendants, gave thanks to God for providing her a ride home. My thoughts, on the other hand, were on the kindness of the driver, who may have jeopardized his job. Rather than focusing on his human act of kindness, everyone focused on God's deliverance.

---

22. A study of fifty older Black women who lived in poverty concludes,

> These properties [of their relationship with God] are: 1) reciprocity, i.e. respondents' covenantal partnership makes them co-actors with God in surviving poverty; they believe they will be liberated from hardship and they view adversity as a forum that displays their personal strength; and 2) familiarity, i.e. their interaction with God is personal, concrete and this-worldly. They are able to talk to God about any major or minor matter in their lives, and in some cases named God as "the person closest to me." Reciprocity and familiarity with God act as a means to cope with hardship because they effect: 1) a sense of *self-worth* based on a belief in God's personal concern, and 2) a conviction that their individual life, however difficult, is part of a *divine plan* that will bring rewards both in this life and the next. Reciprocity and familiarity with God preclude despair and engender hope in the future. They do so by allowing women to *rename adversity as achievement* and to *reframe harsh life circumstances* as enfolded in God's omniscience and personal love.

> Helen K. Black, "Poverty and Prayer: Spiritual Narratives of Elderly African American Women," *Review of Religious Research* 40, no. 4 (June 1999): 364.

Another time, a woman called me to report that someone had just paid for her purchases at the grocery store. She said, laughing, "What is God going to do next?" Again, my thought had been, "What a nice person." In the Prayer Service, we heard a story about a man who had to have work boots for his new job. He decided he would have to shoplift them because he had no money at all. The security guard caught him, and instead of calling the police, the guard paid for the boots. Again, there was great praise for God and what a good God we have. I was also moved by the story, but my mind had immediately gone to the security guard, his motivations, his courage, his kindness.[23]

These disparate attributions for acts of kindness—my attribution to a human agent, theirs to God—are no doubt rooted in differences in access to power. We who are socially located to have greater access to social and economic power live with more experience of our own efficacy. In a social context where there is a great deal less access to worldly power, there is a greater tendency to call upon the power of God, to rely on the power of God when human power is severely restricted. One professional woman who grew up in the Black Church notes, "For [people at UMD], their dependence on God is their only option." Habits of turning to God for protection and provision have been hewn by centuries of having no other choice. When homelessness makes life difficult and complicated, God may intervene through a human agent or otherwise and "make a way out of no way." One woman who was concerned about a place to park her car so that it would be protected from both the police and intruders said, "My savings are utilized. I've been living out of my car. *I have to rely on the Holy Spirit* to know where to go, where to park."

---

23. My church places great emphasis on one's actions as the heart of the life of faith. We are steeped in calls to correct social injustices in order to usher in God's kingdom on earth. If my eyes have been formed to see human actions as the heart of faith, others have been formed to see where God is helping them survive. Furthermore, we progressive Protestants, perhaps especially Presbyterians with our high estimation of education, live in a particularly disenchanted world. The Reformed tradition has a deeply engrained, iconoclastic hesitance to attribute things of this world to God. Our history of struggle with premodern fundamentalists in our camp reinforced our caution regarding naming the spirit of God at work in the everyday world.

However, the religious tradition that predominates at the shelter does not preclude human agency; God does not reduce people to puppets. "Turn it over to the Lord, and you do your part," one person said after describing how he landed a job. Another woman said, "He [God] can't help you if you don't want him to." Sometimes people are God's conduits: "Keep your heart open so the Lord can do what he need to do through you." Another man said plainly, "He's not going to fix nothing on its own. That's why he gives us self-will. He's not going to push it on you, but if you show your trust in him, and believe in that faith, everything else is just going to fall into place." Both partnership and submission are pathways to human agency. "Sometimes we are to do our part in partnership with God, but sometimes we are to simply submit, leaving our will behind." Other times, human agency paradoxically means relinquishing human power in submission to God. Agency may also result from a contract with God. "I pray, and I say, 'God, your will, not mine.' Whatever you say, that's what I'll do, and I humble myself, and *you take care of me; I'll take care of this.*" Sometimes it is a matter of being "used" by God. "I just have to be willing to be open to be used of God. It's just a matter of being willing and open to give of myself and letting God show me how."[24]

Questions of the existence of God have never been raised during my tenure at UMD.[25] Nor have abstract questions of the apparent contradiction between scientific truth and religious truth been part of the discussions. Nor has the question of the reality of an

---

24. *Submission* has been a fraught term for feminists, womanists, and liberationists. Among groups who have been socialized to submit, and who rightfully know their survival is linked to their submission, the affirmation of a submissive posture has been roundly critiqued. Similarly, womanists have criticized the valorization of servanthood. Jacqueline Grant, "The Sin of Servanthood and the Deliverance of Discipleship," in *A Troubling in My Soul: Womanist Perspectives on Evil and Suffering*, ed. Emilie Townes (Maryknoll, NY: Orbis, 1993), 199–217. However, in more recent literature, the multivalent meanings of submission have been made apparent. Some have shown how under the banner of submission, women practice resistance and exercise power. See Griffith, *God's Daughters*, and Mary McClintock Fulkerson's *Changing the Subject: Women's Discourses and Feminist Theology* (Minneapolis: Fortress, 1994).

25. The absence of questions regarding the existence of God may not simply be because they do not arise. It could also be because it is not considered appropriate in the presence of the chaplain. It could also be that "questioning God" results in the withholding of God's blessings.

all-powerful, all-loving God in the midst of evil been asked. God's existence, God and a scientific worldview, and theodicy are issues that are easily contemplated under conditions of privilege. Under conditions of suffering, desperation, and profound deprivation, these philosophical, rational questions seem trite and irrelevant. Discourse about God is not about *believing in God* in the presence of suffering; it is about *trusting in God*, whose reality is undeniable, trusting that God will provide for them. God is unquestionably present in everyday life, and God's existence is not up for debate. According to Timothy Nelson, "God and Satan appeared in these accounts not simply as objects of belief, but as *objects of their everyday experience.* That is, they existed as *agents* [emphasis his] whose actions were perceived to be just as knowable, just as real, and just as consequential in [their] day-to-day lives."[26]

Explanations for suffering include God; they do not call into question the existence of God. "My problem was for disobedience because I wasn't listening to God." Sometimes it is because suffering is making you a better person. "It's just like David; my problem, *my tribulation, was good for me.* So everything David went through, it was good for him because David's problems helped him be strong in the Lord; he had to trust God more." One woman found an explanation for her disability in the biblical creation story. "God would never make you crippled like that. That's from the people. *That's from when Adam and Eve ate the apple; a lot of sins came.* That's where this stuff come from."

In response to a direct question about why bad things happen to good people, one woman did not give an explanation but instead affirmed God's power. To her, theodicy was not called for; rather, evidence of God's provisions was an answer to the question.

God takes what the devil meant for evil, and he turns it around for the good.[27] Because if, see, all my friends had already gone to heaven with Jesus already and had not things gone really

---

26. Nelson, *Every Time I Feel,* 49 (emphasis mine).
27. Cooper-Lewter and Mitchell make the same observation about "soul theology." God "will squeeze from the evil itself a literal blessing." Cooper-Lewter and Mitchell, *Soul Theology,* 15.

terribly bad where I was, I wouldn't be here, where God blessed me with a lot of brothers and sisters in the Lord. And now I have a new circle of friends—'cause all my old friends are up in heaven now. So it was hard to understand at the time why I'm in such a horrible situation. But if I wasn't in that horrible situation, I wouldn't have wind up here in Durham, where I met a whole new circle of friends. So you see what I mean? Yeah, bad things do happen, but it turns out for the better for us.

———

Experiencing God is not about entering another realm, the realm of the sacred or the holy, because God is always present in the world. It is not about leaving the earthly and entering the heavenly. The sacred and the profane are not segregated. God is an ever-present character in one's life here and now. Stories of "divine intervention into every aspect of ordinary life . . . attests to how completely intertwined the spiritual, physical, and social forces are."[28]

Finally, to "put God at the center of my life" is not only about believing in God's existence, nor is it only about an internal orientation toward the divine. It is also about living up to moral requirements: refraining from drug use, cruelty, violence, meanness, selfishness, and spending time with "the wrong crowd." It is about returning to prayer, Bible study, kindness, and generosity. It is all of a piece: connection to God and living a certain way. This is not universal. There are some who say that they felt connected to God for the entire time they were "on the street," but usually, connection to God and moral behavior are one and the same. There is an intrinsically moral, behavioral aspect to a relationship with God.

GRATITUDE

The response to God's activity in our lives is gratitude.

"My friend Michelle is in the hospital. She was shot in the head five times," Andre said from the podium. He always spoke softly

———

28. Nelson, *Every Time I Feel*, 92.

and looked straight ahead, over our heads. This time, he spoke especially slowly. Gasps flew through the room. I was stunned.

My brain was scrambled by Andre's announcement. I was speechless. Something "out there" usually introduced through news reports was now "in here," in the Prayer Service. My only hermeneutic was the abstract category "gun violence." Then immediately after Andre's shocking announcement, I heard from here and there in the room, "Praise God. Thank you, Jesus." I was confused. I thought, "What? What is happening here?" To me, there was a strong dissonance between their reaction and the report of gunshots to the head. Then I heard, "She could have been dead. Praise God." There was consensus among worshippers that this was a praiseworthy report. In the gasp-filled pause between Andre's words and the room's response, my thoughts and theirs went in different directions. I was stuck on the horror; they were fixed on Michelle's survival. In just two or three seconds, "She was shot five times" led to "Praise God." These worshippers had the habit of responding in a particular way: gratitude for what remained. In that same two or three seconds, I was paralyzed.

My conversation with the professional woman unaffiliated with UMD surfaced an additional explanation for this reaction of gratitude. She said they were grateful that God can "take something and turn it around and mean it for good" by using this woman's injuries to encourage others. The story Andre told "will make me look at the situations I'm going through and not complain"; it makes people think, "I know my life could be so much worse," and "when you hear the stories and situations of others who are going through so much worse, it makes you look at your own life and not complain. Instead of complaining, ask God for endurance, perseverance, and strength to overcome whatever it is that you are facing."

In the bleak world of many at UMD, with overwhelming evidence that the world offers them little, it is possible that the turn to gratitude arose out of a refusal to acknowledge yet another reminder of the violent, crushing circumstances of their lives. To take in the reality of the horrific shooting would simply be too crushing, too disabling. So as an emotionally protective measure, there is instead a grasp for a reason to be grateful, some reason to continue to claim God's sovereignty in the face of such powerfully threatening forces. The pivot to gratitude, then, is a way to continue to move through a challenging world without being disabled by its debilitating realities. In the moment's pause, I can imagine their thoughts "descended into hell," and after three seconds, they "rose again from the dead" to give thanks to God.

My lived theological world does not offer habits of gratitude in response to such horror. Thus brain scramble and spiritual freeze were my reactions. In my tradition, we do not have quickly accessible liturgical, spiritual responses to violence that are a part of our shared repertoire. I was mute.

While deeply engrained habits of responding to violence were not within my immediate grasp, if I had had time, I may have encouraged lament in response to the gun violence using the words of the psalmist "How long O Lord . . ." Or I might have said that we should simply keep a silent vigil for Michelle and for a generalized world where violence holds sway. Or I might have invoked Jesus' words "Blessed are the peacemakers" as a call to an alternative way of being in the world, to authorize and empower the group to address violence as peacemakers. While expressions of gratitude for Michelle's survival might have been included, they would not have been my focus. "Praise God" would have been far down my list of pastoral responses.

There are several possible ways to account for the centrality of the habit of gratitude among people at UMD. It could be said that gratitude practices are prevalent because they "work."[29] Among Black women in eastern North Carolina who endured many life difficulties, gratitude was associated with faith that God will provide and give a reprieve from despair.[30] "Faith that God will provide a means for getting food, restoring electricity, or reconnecting the hot water heater gives one strength not to give up when hopelessness seems inevitable. . . . Gratitude in the midst of these circumstances is a reflection of both an expectation of God's blessing and a

---

29. Philip C. Watkins, Michael Van Gelder, and Araceli Frias, "Furthering the Science of Gratitude," in *The Oxford Handbook of Positive Psychology*, ed. Shane J. Lopez and C. R. Snyder, 2nd ed. (New York: Oxford University Press, 2009).

30. Frederick, *Between Sundays*, 63-81. Low-income women interviewed by Susan Crawford Sullivan in the Boston area also included gratitude as a central part of their spirituality. Sullivan, *Living Faith*, 35–37.

realization that God is historically provided for basic needs."[31] Gratitude and hope among these women gave rise to "endurance and therefore the possibility of change in the midst of adversity."[32] Gratitude "works" by fostering endurance and hope for change. Multiple empirical studies claim that gratitude "works" from medical and psychological perspectives. Gratitude and spiritual practices are associated with lower levels of depression and anxiety.[33] Gratitude is associated with better health.[34] Measures of subjective well-being are significantly higher for people who practice gratitude.[35]

It could also be said that there are conservative Evangelical pressures to give thanks in all things because that is the rule: "In every thing give thanks: for this is the will of God in Christ Jesus concerning you" (1 Thess 5:18 KJV). The habit of gratitude emerged in the context of this well-known imperative from the apostle Paul.[36] To fail to give thanks is to question God, to doubt the goodness and power of God. In the Pentecostal tradition, believers even give thanks for what God has not yet done but will most surely do.

People at UMD also dwell in a soup of popular culture that has picked up on the benefits of practicing gratitude. Oprah Winfrey popularized gratitude journals, and she speaks of the "power of gratitude."[37] The interest in Buddhism and meditation, especially

31. Frederick, *Between Sundays*, 71.
32. Frederick, 73.
33. David Rosmarin, Elizabeth J. Krumrei, and Kenneth I. Pargament, "Are Gratitude and Spirituality Protective Factors against Psychopathology?," *International Journal of Existential Psychology & Psychotherapy* 3, no. 1 (2010): 1–5.
34. Kiralee Schache et al., "Gratitude—More Than Just a Platitude? The Science behind Gratitude and Health," *British Journal of Health Psychology* 24, no. 1 (2018): 1–9.
35. For a full exploration of a psychological understanding of gratitude, see Robert A. Emmons and Michael E. McCullough, eds., *The Psychology of Gratitude* (New York: Oxford University Press, 2004).
36. This centrality of this practice of gratitude is not limited to conservative Evangelicals. From a more progressive perspective, Father David Stendl-Rast has widespread impact through his writings and his website: gratefulness.org. As a Benedictine monk, he has been in active dialogue with Buddhism for decades. He has given a TED talk, appeared as a guest on Krista Tippett's *On Being* podcast, and been interviewed by Oprah Winfrey. Among some activist groups, his early book entitled *Gratefulness: The Heart of Prayer* (Ramsey, NJ: Paulist, 1984) has been popular. In reformed theology, the basis for ethical behavior is gratitude for what God has done.
37. Oprah Winfrey, "6 Things We Know for Sure about the Power of Gratitude," Oprah.com, accessed January 11, 2019, https://tinyurl.com/y5ecqlca. According

among "spiritual but not religious" groups, has broadened the understanding of gratitude as a healthy practice.

Whatever the reasons, people at UMD participate in practices of gratitude that are deeply rooted historically and popular in their present situations. It is a core element of prayer and of response to life events, both life-giving and life-taking.

The Devil

"I thank God for many blessings and for breaking strongholds [of the devil]," one woman said. God not only offers blessings for which we should be grateful, but God defeats the efforts of the devil.

The devil is active in the world.[38] The devil tempts people to stray from the right path by luring them to attractive but bad choices, such as drugs or "women." Also, the devil works by throwing obstacles in people's way, such as a late bus or a wallet stolen, making it harder to fulfill commitments or perform tasks.

Often, the devil can be wholly blamed for relapsing or destructive behavior. One woman spoke of her own unwillingness to accept help and said it was all the devil's doing. "That wasn't nobody but the devil trying to keep me from these people. He didn't want me to get no help from them, didn't want them to help me." The devil is also responsible for violence. A spate of stabbings in Durham was attributed to the devil at work in our city. The violence occurred "because the devil is on the rampage. He's seeking who he may devour. He's coming to rob, steal, kill, and destroy."

---

to this website, it is not the gracious *giver* of the gift who evokes gratitude that is powerful; it is the *subjective experience* of gratitude that is powerful.

38. The devil or Satan as a category is not new in American history. For a thorough review of the role of the concept of the devil in church, theology, and popular culture from the colonial era to today, see W. Scott Poole's *Satan in America: The Devil We Know* (Lanham, MD: Rowman & Littlefield, 2009). Many of the strains present throughout American history are present among people at UMD. Poole also shows how the concept of evil has been used against people who might frequent UMD: "Not surprisingly, middle class America and its spokespeople turned to the concept of evil to describe the plight of the poor, the drug-addicted, and the marginalized." Poole, 174.

Yet human autonomy is also recognized when personal responsibility is named. "Sometimes it's not the adversary, sometimes it is us. He [the adversary] can help us [go wrong], but we are the problem." Some, though not all, do speak of "bad choices": "When demons take the place of the Holy Spirit, the devil is in control. I was lost because [of] my bad choices, bad decisions."

One woman reminded me of the belief that acts of faithfulness by believers can trigger the devil's retribution.[39] She said that because we had prayed together for her sister the day before, the devil retaliated by making her sister "pop the pills." Her sister had to go to the hospital, "and then she almost not live; she was talking out of her head. But now she's good 'cause God, he listened; he still heard our prayers, even after the fact that Satan trick her into taking the pills." Our prayers evoked Satan's retaliation.

When we hear of individual destructive behavior in the Prayer Service that is attributed to the devil, the person is not to blame; it is the devil. The explanation for this behavior is, "That ain't nothing but the devil." There is space between the person and the demonic force that has determined their actions. For some people, the category of "devil" allows them to acknowledge their failings while mitigating feelings of personal shame. While this could be a refusal to take responsibility for one's actions, my observation is that people are only too ready to name their failures. Attributing them to an alien spirit within them offers some protection from the painful experience of shame.

In response to disturbing reports of social/political bad behavior on a larger scale, such as gang activity or politicians' corruption or police violence, one person might say, "There's evil spirits out there." It offers an explanation for horrific acts of racism, cruelty, egocentrism, greed, or flat-out evil. I believe it lowers the anxiety of the room. By naming these harmful individuals and social/cultural entities as of the devil, it seems to contain the threat; it reduces the inexplicable and uncontrollable to something that we have survived before and that will be defeated by God. It draws evil into the container of a narrative of God's omnipotent power, which will always prevail.

---

39. Nelson makes a similar point: "Satan will also try harder to tempt those who are successfully advancing God's Kingdom." Nelson, *Every Time I Feel*, 107.

There is also an element of empowerment when speaking of the devil. Among women living in poverty in Boston, the devil as an interpretive scheme "can evoke resilience and strength." It is empowering to resist the devil. Susan Crawford Sullivan says, "Naming their feelings of hopelessness and helplessness as 'of the devil' allows the mothers to categorize such feelings as things that are 'not of God.'" Thus these feelings become "an external enemy against whom women can fight" rather than moods over which they have no power.[40] Similarly, in a study of middle-class women, references to the devil granted them authority: "In choosing to obey God's will rather than give in to Satan's temptations, women are rewarded with the *God-given authority* to banish Satan and to render him virtually powerless."[41] At UMD, references to the devil often serve as a rallying cry, a focus of condemnation. To cast an event as the work of Satan is to marshal the troops for the work of resistance; it unites people.

In any theological world that includes the devil, it is possible to speak of mysterious, invisible, powerful sources of sin and evil. There is a category for speaking of a source of suffering, destruction, and untimely death. Theological progressives, more schooled in the habits of thinking required by a disenchanted world, would be more likely to refer to psychological sources of individual sin and social, political, and economic dynamics as sources of the corporate sin of greed and indifference toward impoverished communities. It is certainly necessary to use these categories to speak of sources of suffering in order to begin to undo them. However, in the final analysis, evil is a mystery beyond all human categories, and referring to it in terms of entities and spirits beyond human ken fits this reality.

The danger, of course, is when evil or the devil is identified with one group or individual, which has happened throughout history, to horrific consequence: infidels during the medieval Crusades, witches in European and American history, or the Jewish people in European history. This identification of the devil with a hated minority results in not only violence and death but also excruciating self-hatred on the part of members of this minority.

---

40. Sullivan, *Living Faith*, 49.
41. Griffith, *God's Daughters*, 193 (emphasis mine). I am indebted to Susan Campbell Sullivan for her reference to this text.

The devil as a category in Christian theology has risks. It is worth noting, though, that the people at UMD experience evil's harshest effects, and they do refer to Satan, the devil, and evil spirits. Before rejecting all references to the devil, some deference to them is due.

PURPOSE: "GOD HAS A PURPOSE FOR ME"

Through all of life's trials, through everything that Satan throws at them, the people at UMD often have confidence that one's suffering is not wasted. One regular attendee at the Prayer Service who had been living at the shelter for several months said, "I know the Lord's got me here [in a homeless shelter] . . . to lift up other people and get them to realize that they need to walk with the Lord and be the light. I try to be an encouragement and bring God's word to light." She does not ascribe her stay in the homeless shelter to her own failure or worthlessness, but rather, it is part of God's good plan to bring others to God and to encourage them.

One of the surprises in my interviews and participant observation has been the number of people who have reported either nearly dying or actually dying. Recounting the story of her illness, one woman said, "When they put that shunt in me [and] it didn't work, I went blind for four months. . . . I've been dead three times. *Why do you think you are still alive?* Because I got something else to do." God preserves a person's life for a purpose. "I was on the operating table. I died three times. Each time they brought me back, I seen the face of God and the young lady that took me there from the prison camp. Like I said, I died three times, and I'm sixty-eight years old. Right here still doing. He kept me here for a reason. God blesses."

One man who spent many years in prison experienced interior growth in order to be equipped to do God's work when he was released.

———

I'm supposed to have been dead a long time ago. *Why do you say that?* Because there've been riots in the prisons and in the hallways, and I'm standing right there, and people next to me are being stabbed. And you can hear the shank go through the person and hitting the back of the wall. And people that's on the floor that's being stabbed, and you can hear it going through them and hitting the floor. And I'm walking out without a scratch. . . . I believe I reached some levels of consciousness. I believe that I went through everything that I went through for a reason. I reached some level of consciousness that I probably would never realize . . . that I never would have realized being out here because it was almost like I was set into prison with my eyes wide to see everything that was going on to come back out *to be able to, I guess, do whatever is his business.* (emphasis mine)

———

His survival was not attributed to his particular intelligence or to random luck, but it was because he had to "do God's business."

Often connected to the affirmation that God brought a person back from the dead, or kept them alive under difficult circumstances, is the claim that "God has a purpose for my life" or God has "something he wants me to do" or "a reason for me to be here."

———

I struggle and something good happens for me, and then I go right back down. I just never gave up, you know? I'm here for a reason. Everybody's here for a reason. I really believe that. God ain't gonna put you on this earth and keep you living for nothing. He's got something in store for everybody.

———

A woman who had survived a violent marriage also attributed her survival to God having a purpose for her.

———

Like my pastor told me, "You should have been dead. You were supposed to be dead." . . . I mean, my husband beat me. We were together three years; he didn't put his hands on me. Soon as I married him, he started beating on me. Threw me off the balcony, broke my tailbone, burned my breast with a cigarette. He drug me through the house and beat my head on the floor. I have seizures now. I'm telling you, he did some damage to me. "It's his [God's] purpose," my dad always told me. You have a purpose to be here.

Believing that suffering has a purpose can enable survival and hope. It draws pain into a larger schema of God's transformative activity on earth, the triumph of good over evil, the participation in something larger than one's own small, difficult world. It is a means of transcending the often grim details of life lived without a home. It is a way of conceiving of oneself as valuable beyond what external evidence might suggest. Giving meaning to hardship is widely known to fund survival.[42] Meaning making and purpose finding are useful in conditions of chronic pain.[43] Among survivors of combat, those who have experienced the trauma of warfare, it is found that meaning making strengthens coping skills.[44] One research group found that "the generation of meaning and purpose in life are important variables that relate to positive adaptation following spinal cord injury."[45] The painful process of making meaning after trauma helps "restore a sense of the world as meaningful and their own lives as worthwhile."[46]

------

42. "Meaning" can be understood in two ways: One, "positive value or purpose," as in the belief that one's suffering will bear fruit; it is not meaningless suffering. The other meaning is "interpretation," where suffering could be interpreted as useless, or an inevitable part of human life, or punishment of the gods, but not necessarily bearing positive value or purpose. I am speaking of "meaning making" as constructing a positive value or purpose for one's experience.

43. Jessie Dezutter, Laura Dewitte, and Siebrecht Vanhooren, "Chronic Pain and Meaning in Life: Challenge and Change," in *Meanings of Pain*, ed. Simon van Rysewyk (Cham, Switzerland: Springer, 2016).

44. Brad Larner and Adrian Blow, "A Model of Meaning-Making, Coping and Growth in Combat Veterans," *Review of General Psychology* 15, no. 3 (2011): 187–97.

45. Terri A. deRoon-Cassini et al., "Psychological Well-Being after Spinal Cord Injury: Perception of Loss and Meaning Making," *Rehabilitation Psychology* 54, no. 3 (2009): 306–14.

46. C. L. Park, "Trauma and Meaning Making: Converging Conceptualizations and Emerging Evidence," in *The Experience of Meaning in Life: Classical Perspectives, Emerging Themes, and Controversies*, ed. J. Hicks and C. Routledge (Dordrecht, Netherlands: Springer, 2013), 61.

Claiming a purpose for their lives is a way to claim that their suffering will not have the last word. Good will arise from it. Evil will not prevail.

Personal Prayer

In order to receive God's blessings, and to be protected from the devil's works, prayer is essential. Prayer is by far the most frequently mentioned religious practice. This is true for all Americans, but prayer is more frequent among Blacks and people at the lowest income levels.[47] It is a way to access God and to fight off the devil that does not require a particular place, a particular appearance, or particular possessions. Prayer is a religious practice that can take place at any time, at any place, under any circumstances. Almost everyone I interviewed said they pray first thing in the morning. Many said they thank God for surviving through the night. Many speak of praying before they fall asleep, and several spoke of praying all day long. When I asked one person when she prays, she said, "All the time. When I'm walking down the street. I don't care what I'm doing. I sit there with my inner peace and pray." One mother said, "I pray all the time. Especially when I'm by myself. [My son] be in the room watching TV. I pray, and I cry, especially at church when they say, like, everything you been through, God is always been there. And he's always going to be there." People gave thanks when things were going well, asked for deliverance when things were not, and began and ended the day with prayer, and many simply spoke to God as they moved through the day. These prayers bespoke a relationship of familiarity and intimacy with God.

When I asked one person what he said in his prayers, he said he was not only in constant prayer, but prayer got him through the day.

---

47. See "Religious Landscape Study," Pew Research Center, accessed January 15, 2019, https://tinyurl.com/yaontunx; and "Prayer in America," Pew Research Center, accessed January 15, 2019, https://tinyurl.com/y3f3hs4u.

———

And when I'm walking around, I sometimes keep [saying], "Jesus I need you, Jesus." And sometimes I might walk somewhere, and I'm saying, "Jesus I need you. I need you in my heart today. Just help me get through this day." And I end my prayer. And I say, "I send this prayer to you through your son Jesus Christ, Amen." So that's how I pray.

———

Prayer can be a means to overcome a sense of being alone in a difficult situation, as this woman told me.

———

Whenever I get in my troublesome moments, I know who to call on. Like, I know it's just not me alone, by myself, that I do have a higher power. *And what kinds of things do you say?* "God, I need you; help me, like, help me get out of this situation. I'm going to wait on you." I talk to him as if he was a human. I spend time with the Lord in my alone time in prayer, and the spirit of God in me ministers to me.

———

Others' prayers are efficacious and can provide protection from harm.

———

Somebody's watching out for me. Somebody's doing some praying. Somebody's looking out for me. It can't be coincidence. Sometimes it's like some guy that got killed in a car accident, and I was supposed to be there. And I get a little gnawing in the back of my head, "Don't, don't, don't go. Don't go." [I said,] "I ain't going, y'all; go ahead." "Come on, man, come on. We coming right back." "OK." And I'm walking toward the car, and there's something in my gut saying, "You don't want to do this." "You all go ahead, man. I'm just going to hang out right here." And the closer I get to going, the more gnawing the feeling is. "Y'all go." And when they leave, I feel better. And then I hear later on that they been in an accident, and everybody in the car died. And I keep saying, that's not coincidence. [*long pause*] And I don't know of many people that can go to prison twice, and at the young age that I start out with, and not be raped or killed or come out unscathed. I'm not talking about juvenile detention. I'm talking about straight to the big house.

———

Prayer can also be a means of relinquishing control and allowing God to work. One man had paid in advance for several weeks in a hotel, and then he was blocked from reentering because he had entertained visitors. His assessment was "It's a demonic system we are living in." He called the police, and rather than helping him recover the advance payment that he lost, the police only offered to accompany him to the room to pick up his belongings. "They acted like I was the criminal," he said.

Then the man prayed, saying, "So I want you, Lord, to take charge." He left the hotel and went to the Veterans Administration (VA) hospital, hoping he could sleep there. However, he was not allowed to sleep there even though he told the VA staff he was "manic-depressive" and he "might hurt somebody." In spite of being turned away from two places to sleep that night, "I wasn't worried. I knew I had to stay in prayer. I remembered that saying 'If you pray, don't worry; if you worry, don't pray.' So I had total peace over me." It was warm that night and he slept outside, and then the next night, the temperature dropped below freezing, and he was allowed to sleep in the shelter. Soon, he was offered an apartment. He concluded, "I changed my whole outlook on God. I have to get out of the way and let him do his work."

Not only did he get an apartment quicker than usual, but even the weather cooperated: the temperature dropped below freezing, and the shelter put out a white flag, meaning everyone can come in for the night. All of these fortunate events happened because he decided to "get out of the way and let [God] do his work."

Rather than praying simply that God's will be done in a general sense or praying that they will have the strength to get through whatever it is that befalls them, the prayers are often for a very specific outcome. While one woman was in a drug rehabilitation program and her children were dispersed to various places to live, she deeply desired that they be reunited as a family.

———

All I did was pray the whole time. "I know you are going to look out for me; I know you are going to get my kids back. I'm going to be patient." And I got all my kids back. You know, I just prayed on it. I just prayed on it and prayed on it and prayed on it. Then, one by one, all my kids started coming home. One by one. And I said, "God is good all the time."

———

The return of her children, one by one, was all God's doing, prompted by her prayer.

Another man prayed for God to teach him how to be merciful when he has been mistreated instead of trying to extract justice. He prayed for two hours that he might be given a spirit of mercy instead of vengeance.

———

I'll tell you my greatest foe: being able to forgive and turn the other cheek. . . . If the day was to come for someone to spit in my face, what would I do? How would I react? . . . If it's somebody I could easily beat up? . . . *Today I'm trying to pray, and I'm trying to learn to ask for mercy and not justice* because I was given mercy.

———

One woman reported that God had helped remove her desire to communicate with a man with whom she did not want to be involved.

———

I had met this guy, and I was really so into him. I mean, he was just everything. And I asked the Lord, "Please help me back up from this man because I know he's not going to be the right one." And he helped me. He really, really helped me, because I didn't want to call him as much. I didn't want to text him, and now I don't even text or call him.

———

However, it was recognized that prayers aren't always answered exactly as desired: "I just pray and ask for what I need. I don't ask for what I want; I ask for what I need, and sure enough, I got what I need because my housing came through."

Timing is another factor in fulfilling a prayer request. A reason offered for an unfulfilled prayer, or a delayed fulfillment, is that God's timing is not always our timing.

———

He answers prayers all the time. Sometimes he says yes, sometimes he says no, and sometimes he says, "Not right now." But what we have to do is find the ability to accept the decisions that he make. What we do is ask for his will. It doesn't matter what we like or dislike; what matters is what is God's will and can we find both the courage and the willingness to carry that out. And that's what I'm trying to work with.

———

The task of the believer, then, is to "find both the courage and the willingness" to do God's will.

Prayer is a practical response to personal ills. During the Prayer Service, another woman spoke of pain in her leg and feeling discouraged and depressed. Immediately, people started speaking words of encouragement, each having to do with prayerful interactions with God.

———

Keep your mind on Jesus, take your mind off yourself, and trust God.

Worship and praise God; let him control things you can't control.

Turn it over to Jesus, and he will make everything all right.

Acknowledge him in all your ways, and he shall direct thy path.

———

Prayer is the most important individual practice of personal piety, and it plays an important role in perseverance, hope, and equanimity.

BIBLE READING

Prayer and Bible study are often mentioned together. The Bible is by far the piece of material culture in their religious lives that I see most frequently. Individual Bible reading, "staying in my Bible," is usually without an aid such as a study book. In the Prayer Service, the most common readings offered by participants are from the Psalms. "I love everything about the Bible. I just love it," one person said. Several people reported that reading the Bible has the powerful effect of improving their mood. "If you pick up the Bible, and you are going through something, and you read some passages, it'll make you feel so good" or "When I go to the Prayer Service or read the Bible, I don't know, they make me feel good." When I asked how one woman knew what to read in the Bible, she said, "I just open up that Bible and ask God to point a page to me. And that's what I do. I just read it."

For some, the Bible functions as an icon, a piece of the material world that links the believer to God. Once, I was talking to a man who had been living in his van, which was parked on the street next to UMD, and he said he had a Bible "in his bag." I asked one person why he carried a Bible with him. He said, "To read and hold on to. A symbol of God. A symbol of God. . . . Like a tabernacle. . . . That's my tabernacle; that's my, you know, that's my freedom. I mean, you can't get no more peace than that, when you got a Bible." The Bible reading itself can be efficacious;

it "can work." He told me, "I know it's going to work, whatever it is, 'cause it's the Bible."

In a similar vein, one woman spoke of putting her Bible under her pillow so she could sleep.

———

People ask me all the time why I keep my Bible under my pillow. I sleep on my Bible only because . . . if I have my Bible next to me, I feel I am safe. I don't feel safe if it's not with me. I left my Bible in storage for a week because I moved from house to house. I didn't want to lose it. I felt so bad, so many bad things. When I was coming here, I said, "I must take my Bible because if I don't take it, how will I be able to go back to sleep?" I been having a hard time sleeping, be having nightmares and bad dreams. And now my dreams have been good since I been laying back on my Bible, sleeping back on it. A week without it, I been having nightmares, bad dreams, people dying in my dreams, stuff happening that I don't like. I had to read the Word to get back to sleep again.[48]

———

When asked about reading the Bible, one particular man explained that he had difficulty with being able to read, but miraculously, he could read the Bible. He said, "I can read the words in the Bible. That's very strange. The Lord blessed me to read the Bible."

When I was a student in a practical theology PhD seminar in the nineties, I spoke of the need for psychotherapy to treat depression. A fellow student responded with intensity: "Do you know what has helped Black people survive?" He held up his Bible and

---

48. It is possible that the affirmation of the Bible as bearing peace and a sense of safety is linked to a literalist interpretation of Scripture, which offers a sense of certainty. One ethnographic study showed a tendency toward fundamentalism in a group of Black seminary and college students. The researchers conclude that this "orientation may meet a psychosocial need for certainty and stability when faced with change and uncertainty. . . . Such orientation could represent a form of agency and self-empowerment." Velma E. Love, "Scriptures as Sundials in African American Lives," in *MisReading America: Scriptures and Difference*, ed. Vincent L. Wimbush (New York: Oxford University Press, 2013), 94.

said, "This. This is what has gotten us through our dark times. We don't have psychotherapy in Harlem; we have the Bible." A fruitful conversation ensued, and we both grew. This conversation underscored the deep historical, therapeutic, healing significance of the Bible for many Blacks. This fact is apparent in the reverence for the physical Bible at UMD and in the fact that it is almost the only piece of religious material culture that is retained by people living without shelter. Other material objects do function as vehicles to the holy, such as a photo or a laminated card with an inspirational saying, but the Bible is virtually the only part of traditional religious material culture that is retained.

Music

Some of the girls [in the dorm] walk around singing Jesus songs and God songs and stuff like that, and that gives me inspiration. I look at them, and they are just as happy as they want to be. And so I get a lot of inspiration from them.

Music adds a communal element to spirituality. It draws people together. Some of the people at UMD are very good musicians, especially on the keyboard and the guitar. There are also very skilled vocalists, such as William.

William was one of the first people I met at the shelter. A black patch covered the space where his left eye had been, and he was short, sturdy, compact, and friendly. He almost always sang when he came to the Prayer Service. He did not sing a recognizable selection from the archives of church music or contemporary gospel. Instead, he sang with feeling and flourish a song that he was making up on the spot. They were about God's salvation, praise for God, and staying faithful. "I love to sing," he said. "That most of my joy. Because when I sing, [its] about the Lord, what the Lord done for me. I sing about how my day went. . . . It's the feeling that come over me, and I sing about it." He would close his eye and, with his chin uplifted, sing in a gravelly, high voice. Sometimes he would spontaneously sing when we ran into each other in the parking lot.

He was born in the mid-sixties, grew up in Durham, and started getting high when he was twenty-five years old. Within a few years, he was shot in the head and lost his eye. His heart stopped during surgery, and though people told him the doctor brought him back from the edge, he knew it was God. The drug use was hard on his kidneys. He began dialysis three times a week. But he testified that God did not abandon him.

———

When I used to sit out there and get high, there be a Christian person walk up to me and say, "The Lord sent me to you." And I'm sitting there high on drugs, but I don't leave. I listen. And I can feel the Lord in me. "Is this where you want to be? Is this how you want to be?" It bring tears and I get to crying, asking myself, "Why are you doing this to yourself? You have much more to live for, you know."

———

Over the years, he would come and go from life at the shelter. His health got worse. One time, he stood in the crowded waiting room getting a number for his turn to receive food or clothing. His abdomen was bloated like a large beach ball; his face was puffy. His shoulders looked narrow and thin and his head small. He said he was overdue on his dialysis.

The last time I saw him, I asked if I could interview him. There was something evanescent about him, as though his skin was becoming thin or his substance was thinning, becoming transparent. His voice was especially hoarse and raspy. He would die shortly after this conversation, and he may have known it. He had awakened from a dream in the hospital that morning.

———

When I woke up this morning, no pain. I said, "Thank you, Father. Because if it wasn't for you, you know." My dreams. It's like somewhere in a sort of land, somewhere with pretty flowers and everything. I wake up and I'm in the hospital. I'm like, "Where did this dream come from?" It's warm sunshine; birds fly. What kind of dream is that? I ask God, "Is this where you have me to be?" I'm praying to get out of Durham. Been in Durham all my life. I want a newer place. When my time come, I know that the Lord is ready for me to come home. I'm going to be an angel for somebody. [*choked up*] Excuse me; it's a lot of joy.

———

Some of the stories I tell in this book bring me joy in the telling, some make me intensely curious about the world in which they occurred, and some fill me with awe at the "Godness" of them. They breathe out the Holy Spirit, and I breathe it in during the writing. But some stories are hard to tell. They evoke pain in the telling. The story of William is one of them. I wonder where he died, whether he was with anyone. Did he die into the dream of pretty flowers, warm sunshine, and birds, into a home where the Lord was ready for him? Our connection over time, watching his deterioration, and witnessing his sustained gratitude to God made this a hard story to tell.

SURPRISING SCARCITIES

There are several surprises in my experience as a chaplain and a researcher. For example, God is invoked far more often than Jesus. Only rarely do I hear any reference to an Anselmian understanding of atonement, references to sins washed away by the blood of Jesus, or Jesus's sacrifice for us, or what Jesus did for us on the cross.[49] The absence of these understandings of salvation through Jesus is surprising in the Evangelical South, a tradition that has been characterized as particularly blood soaked in its Christology.

---

49. I have heard a very few long expositions on precisely how Jesus saved us from our sins. My notes show only three occasions when these discourses occurred, and they were from two white women and one white man.

References to giving one's life to Jesus in order to be saved were by no means common occurrences.

There have been very, very few references to the sacraments. Even though many of the worshippers come from a revivalist culture, which emphasizes baptism as a mark of being saved, I have heard of baptism only a couple of times in the service. The absence of the sacrament of Communion is not as surprising in an area where most congregations are from a Low Church tradition.

While I am convinced that references to the devil's work in the world are a form of power analysis of unjust social structures, I have only heard twice of any indication of an explicit social analysis of poverty and hardship, and these references were from men with a college education. Nor do I hear about working for social justice as a matter of faith: poverty, poor health care, bad schools, mass incarceration, or high unemployment as social problems that call for a prophetic response. There are practically no references to racism, sexism, or classism. While there is likely self-censorship around topics of white racism in my presence, it is surprising that I have neither heard in passing nor overheard any references to it. Problems are explained through self-blame (drugs, alcohol, uses of violence) and other-blame (abusive parents, abandonment, cheating spouse, selfish relatives, thieving friends, the devil). They mostly turn on themselves, turn on each other, or point to the devil as an explanation for life problems. However, the category of "sin" is rarely invoked, nor is the need to confess one's sins.

I had expected to hear references to the exodus, God's great event of liberation from oppression. This may be because they did not want to speak explicitly of the oppression of Blacks in my presence either because I am an outsider and I would not understand or be judgmental or because this way of speaking bears a holiness that should only be used in certain holy spaces. They may have thought it would be disrespectful to me or create a distance between them and me. Another reason may be because the exodus is primarily a motif used in corporate worship, not individual piety, and the Prayer Service is a space of personal devotion.[50]

---

50. Many scholars of Black religion have noted the centrality of the exodus as an orienting, guiding motif in the Black Church preaching and worship. Thomas Hoyt Jr. says, "The story of the Exodus speaks especially to blacks. We know the story of the

These are the pieces, fragments, that people at UMD bring with them into the experience of dislocation. Under very difficult circumstances, these pieces sustain, explain, and anchor. They provide a means of connecting not only to the divine but also to each other as they are offered up in the Prayer Service in moments of pain, gratitude, and confusion. If many people arrive at the shelter with few material and relational resources, there are some who also bring with them archives of beliefs, habits, memories, and embodied knowledge from their religious backgrounds.[51]

Cross-Cultural Pastoral Care

These archives of beliefs and practices are not always familiar to the pastoral caregiver from a different background. The work of offering

---

exodus is chiefly the reflection of the activity of God in the life of a people, with the supreme example of that activity being manifested with the Exodus of God's chosen people from slavery in Egypt. This activity of God in their affairs provided the core of the confessions they made when *gathered there for worship*." Hoyt, "Interpreting Biblical Scholarship for the Black Church Tradition," in *Stony the Road We Trod: African American Biblical Interpretation*, ed. Cain Hope Felder (Minneapolis: Augsburg Fortress, 1991), 30 (emphasis mine). David Kling reminds us that James Cone in his early work used Exodus imagery: "As Cone put it in his pioneering study *A Black Theology of Liberation* (1970), 'By delivering this people [the Israelites] from Egyptian bondage and inaugurating the covenant on the basis of that historical event, God reveals that he is the God of the oppressed, involved in their history, liberating them from human bondage. . . . God, because he is the God of the oppressed, takes sides with black people.'" Kling, *The Bible in History: How the Texts Have Shaped the Times* (New York: Oxford University Press, 2006), 226 (brackets in the original), quoting James H. Cone, *A Black Theology of Liberation* (Philadelphia: Lippincott, 1970), 2. See also Cleophus LaRue, "The Exodus as Paradigmatic Text in the African American Community," in *Reclaiming the Imagination: The Exodus as Paradigmatic Narrative for Preaching*, ed. Dave Bland and David Fleer (St. Louis: Chalice, 2009), 119–28; and Kenyatta Gilbert, *Exodus Preaching: Crafting Sermons about Justice and Hope* (Nashville: Abingdon, 2018). However, a focus on the exodus is not what I have observed in the personal piety displayed in Prayer Service as participants give meaning to their suffering and offer encouragement to each other.

51. Shelton and Emerson in *Blacks and Whites* offer a descriptive summary of Black Protestantism in the form of "building blocks." These building blocks are an emphasis on the *experiential* over the doctrinal, they enable *survival*, they appreciate *mystery*, *miracles* are part of everyday life, and a commitment to *justice* is intrinsic to Black Protestantism. Shelton and Emerson, *Blacks and Whites*, 8.

pastoral care is challenging when both *styles* of communication and *archives* of meaning are unfamiliar. To speak the truth of pain and the truth of God's love across cultural, communicative, and power divides is difficult, and some might say it is impossible. In churches in which I was formed, the challenge is often how to offer hope and comfort in a way that does not violate such modernist assumptions as "God does not magically remove human suffering," "God does not intervene in the laws of nature," and "God works within our 'scientific' understanding of the way things work." However, at UMD, believers begin with the assumption that God is powerful and active in the world on our behalf, and the skilled, timely, and fitting assertion of that truth is the appropriate response. Often, the question at the shelter is not, Do you understand me and my pain, and are you with me in it? Rather, it is, Is God going to deliver me?

The beliefs I describe here are not magic words that inevitably produce positive results. They are religious categories and practices that are subject to corruption in the way that any finite good is. The pastoral caregiver may sense that a belief or a practice mediates that which is not of God, such as shame, resignation, despair, or interpersonal hostility. For example, the habit of gratitude can force denial of what is truly hurtful or damaging, or the category of "devil" can be projected on a disliked person in a way that deepens hatred or violence.

When considering a particular belief of a care receiver, pastoral caregivers do well to ask themselves, Does this way of interpreting their situation or construing God disclose God's grace and mercy, or does it occlude the presence of God? Do beliefs "help people connect with goodness and the love of God in themselves, in others, and in the world around them?"[52] Furthermore, does it "help them bear the weight of their suffering?"[53] Does this testimony of God's presence in their lives open them to grace or cause feelings of shame? Some have used a profession of faith in God's healing power as a way to avoid mental health care: "I'm trusting in God." I spoke earlier of Malcolm, who carried a dual diagnosis of substance

---

52. Carrie Doehring, *The Practice of Pastoral Care: A Postmodern Approach*, rev. and expanded ed. (Louisville, KY: Westminster John Knox, 2015), 103–4.
53. Doehring, 104.

use disorder and a mental illness and who decapitated his father and who regularly declared in song that only the righteous will see God. I wondered how this piece of religious tradition served his feeling of peace before God. One Black woman was interviewed for a study in spirituality, sexuality, and the lingering effects of abuse among Black women, and her words reveal the contradiction that religion was "a needed resource in their day-to-day survival . . . [and] also a source of confusion, pain, and longing for acceptance."[54]

In these instances, the pastoral caregiver can, over time, become a "story companion." We can "accept an invitation to accompany another in the unfolding story of a life and to witness to the interwoven threads of divine love."[55] As the story is told over and over again, it becomes possible for the pastoral caregiver to gently ask questions that might obliquely offer an alternative view of God or events that evoke shame, guilt, or paralysis. An alternative to a problematic belief or faith posture may be offered as the caregiver makes "I wonder" statements or offers evidence from the care receiver's life that affirms a more life-giving perspective. Pastoral caregivers have done this for centuries, and working in a cross-cultural situation does not eliminate the responsibility to address harmful beliefs.

Another challenge is when the beliefs that nurture a care receiver conflict with the chaplain's beliefs. For example, when a person affirms the idea that their metastatic cancer is serving God's purposes, or God has a reason for it, that belief conflicts with mine. While I affirm that God can transform suffering to bring out of it some good, most suffering is meaningless, useless, and without good purpose. However, I recognize that when financial, social, and medical resources are not likely forthcoming and God is the only reliable presence in the life of a suffering person, it is deeply sustaining to trust that all events in human life are unfolding according to God's purposes. I recognize that my belief arises from a place of privilege, a place of relative security and freedom from want. I am not grasping for some purpose or meaning for my suffering in order

---

54. Phillis Isabella Shepherd, "Womanist Pastoral Theology and Black Women's Experience of Gender, Religion, and Sexuality," in *Pastoral Theology and Care: Critical Trajectories in Theory and Practice*, ed. Nancy J. Ramsay (Hoboken, NJ: John Wiley & Sons, 2018), 136.

55. Karen D. Scheib, *Pastoral Care: Telling the Stories of Our Lives* (Nashville: Abingdon, 2016), 96.

to have a reason to keep living or to give me the fortitude to make it through another night sleeping outside. I can lightly speak of the meaninglessness of suffering while resting comfortably in my home. Thus I recognize the importance of a degree of humility and deference while caring for people at UMD, always asking the question of context and the need for survival, hope, and resistance.

Furthermore, there is also the question of whether empathy is always the most efficacious pastoral response.[56] There are times in the Prayer Service when the most effective response is the boldly asserted imperative to "keep your mind on Him and He will keep you in perfect peace" (based on Isa 26:3). It is the unwavering proclamation of truths delivered in a particular idiom that evokes the deepest responses from the people gathered. Much training in pastoral care and counseling emphasizes the centrality of empathy, not the skilled deployment of well-known, much-loved sayings, proverbs, and Scripture texts. Thus unfamiliarity with these sayings and the effective delivery of them may hamper cross-cultural pastoral care. Knowledge of the power of this mode of bringing encouragement and assurance of God's power in their lives is important for chaplains working with people similar to the people at UMD.

I hope to produce a profound respect for these archives of texts and practices in the survival of people on the margins, a respect manifest in the way we offer pastoral care. Thus attempts to tinker with beliefs and practices with which we are unfamiliar in our well-meaning pastoral care should be done only with great carefulness. Our often-preferred pastoral language about "living with uncertainties," the "ambiguities" of life, the "ultimately unknowability" of God, and "tolerating a season of disorientation" may not sustain people who fear for their very survival. When the rain starts and the cardboard you are sleeping on gets mushy, when waking up in a place where crack is used regularly and you have no clothes on, when riding the bus in a loop because you have nowhere else to go

---

56. Even if empathy is possible, there remains potential for harmful misunderstanding. According to Melinda A. McGarrah Sharp, "A key postcolonial question is whether any of us can ever see that which we ourselves render invisible. . . . As we begin to recognize cultural and religious pluralism more deeply, how do we face the risk that our own caring practices inadvertently harm the very human beings for whom we intend to care?" Sharp, *Misunderstanding Stories: Toward a Postcolonial Pastoral Theology* (Eugene, OR: Pickwick, 2013), 141.

and no plans for the future, when sleeping in a car with your four children, the deployment of the texts and practices I describe can be deeply sustaining. People in these situations are mostly not wrestling with the questions of theodicy, or the congruence of religion and science, or logical inconsistencies in religious claims.[57] Rather, they are crying out to God for strength to survive, for a solid basis for hope. Their beliefs and practices arise from a well-developed archive that has sustained people in dire straits over the centuries, and it requires respect in our pastoral caregiving.

---

57. Miguel De La Torre says, "When people live under oppressive structures, they turn to the Bible for the strength to survive another day. . . . The Bible is not read with the intellectual curiosity of solving cosmic mysteries; rather; most people on the margins look to the text to find guidance in dealing with daily life, a life usually marked by struggles and hardships." De La Torre, *Reading the Bible from the Margins* (Maryknoll, NY: Orbis, 2002), 40.

CHAPTER 4

RESISTANCE NARRATIVES

The idea that "I have a story to tell" or that it is common to "tell my story" circulates among people at the shelter. Giving an honest account of one's life in a safe environment is a familiar practice. Many churches have traditions of testimony, twelve-step programs include telling one's story, and often therapeutic groups include storytelling.[1] The practice of sharing personal stories for a particular purpose is in the cultural soup of the shelter. Occasionally, people refused my invitations to be interviewed, and it was not always because of privacy concerns or shyness. The reason they gave was that "this is *my* story," implying, "if anybody is going to profit from it, it will be me." Their story held currency, value, and they asserted the right to retain ownership of it.

THE ADDICTION STORY

There are a few identifiable plots common to the stories people tell of their lives.[2] An addiction story often begins with an account of

---

1. According to George H. Jenson, Alcoholics Anonymous (AA) altered the purpose of telling stories from the Oxford movement, in which it originated. If telling stories was part of the Oxford movement's goal to "save the world and create saints," AA stories were about "accepting one's imperfections." Jensen, *Storytelling in Alcoholics Anonymous: A Rhetorical Analysis* (Carbondale: Southern Illinois University Press, 2000), 27. I do not know if the people whose stories are told in this chapter ever attended any twelve-step programs, but this tradition is well known among people at Urban Ministries of Durham (UMD), and it is likely that strands of this storytelling tradition affect the way they tell their stories.
2. The three people whose stories are told in this chapter have all, at some point in their lives, struggled with a substance use disorder. The relationship between homelessness

their *childhood*; it may have been healthy or abusive. Then a *reason* is offered for beginning to use drugs. It may be to belong, to manage symptoms of depression or anxiety, to dull the pain of grief or abuse, or to join in the fun. Then the *consequences* of drug use are outlined: stealing from loved ones, incarceration, or homelessness. Then there is a story of *transformation*, an account of how they turned toward recovery. Finally, there is a statement of the *present* situation, which might be successful recovery or relapse with the hope of returning to a recovery program or continued use without an intention of stopping. When I worked in the women's prison, the plot for telling an addiction story often included childhood sexual abuse. The plot went something like this: "I was sexually abused as a girl. I felt deep shame, so I started using drugs to numb the pain. Then I started stealing to sustain my habit. Now I am in prison."[3] The "sexual abuse to prison pipeline" for girls involved in the juvenile justice system is all too real.[4]

A highly respected member of the Urban Ministries of Durham (UMD) staff shared with me a paper he had written for a class at the community college. It is a story of a substance use disorder and recovery that illustrates a common addiction and recovery story plot.

Lamar

I'll start my story at the age of fourteen. I was intelligent, athletic and, if I may say so myself, had a promising future ahead of me. All

and substance abuse is complicated. Sometimes it is a substance use disorder that led to homelessness, and sometimes it is the pain and stress of not having a home that leads to using drugs and alcohol as a form of self-medication. Sometimes there is an underlying mental illness in both situations. In my experience, at least half of the people who have participated in the Prayer Service have had a period in their lives when drug and alcohol use posed problems. However, it is clear that not all people experiencing homelessness have a substance use disorder, and I would not want to imply by my choice of stories in this chapter that homelessness equals addiction. See Eugenia Didenko and Nicole Pankratz, "Substance Use: Pathways to Homelessness? Or a Way of Adapting to Street Life?," *Visions Journal* 4, no. 1 (2007): 9–10.

3. Dana D. DeHart, "Pathways to Prison: Impact of Victimization in the Lives of Incarcerated Women," *Violence against Women* 14, no. 12 (December 2008): 1362–81. This article includes qualitative data from interviewing sixty incarcerated women and explores the connection between women's trauma and the crimes they committed.

4. Malika Saada Saar et al., "The Sexual Abuse to Prison Pipeline: The Girls' Story," Center for Poverty and Inequality, Georgetown University Law Center.

of which took a side street because I wanted to fit in so bad that I began to experiment with drugs.

Nineteen sixty-eight, I landed a job bagging grocery at the neighborhood store next to my house. The youngest person working there and somewhat of a nerd, I easily gave in to the temptation of alcohol and marijuana to fit in. Well, I'll tell you that in six years, I fitted in so good that I was selling grass, and everyone wanted to be like [me]. Eventually, pot gave way to acid or LSD, hash, speed, and an increasing amount of alcohol.

In 1974, I fathered my first child but was nowhere near being a father. I dropped out of college, and I convinced myself I was doing it to raise my son. I dropped out because I meet a guy who had me selling weed, and I was making $500 a week. So I rationalized that if I stayed in school and graduated that I would be lucky to land a job that paid me what I was already making. As the quality of pot increased and the amount I smoked did the same, my son and his mother no longer mattered. She left, taking William Jr. with her. It was 1976.

Between all of this, I fathered another child in 1975. A daughter, Sharika. This time, I said, "I will not lose the chance to raise my child." So I married her mother. I was twenty-one. Again, the drugs that had progressed to cocaine made me put family, job, and self-respect on the back burner. My wife didn't leave me. I abandoned my family.

For the next thirty years, I only lived for empty sex, drugs, and alcohol. I ruined all that I was and all that I could have become. The golden boy of 1968 had long since lost his shine. The last half of the last thirty years eventually led me to crack, the end of all ends. There was virtually nothing that I wouldn't do or did to attain a crack high.

My mother passed and left me $6,000. I smoked it up in six months. My father passed and left me a house and property and money to the range of $18,000 in cash. The money was gone in a year, and I was living in a house with no water and lights. My sister died and left me $250,000. In five years, the house, land, and money was gone.

The last nine years was spent in rooms, cars, parks, and one-day motels. It was in one of these motels that I asked God to help me or let me die. The fact that I'm writing this story attests to the fact that he didn't let me die.

After approximately thirty-eight years of alcohol, drugs, and a ruinous life, I bottomed out and started the long journey back to sanity and some resemblance of a normal life. I'm clean and sober for one year and two and a half months. Although they are adults, my daughter and son have welcomed me into their lives. I have eight grandchildren, whom I love dearly, and I cherish the ground they walk or crawl on.

[It is] 2009, and now I'll tell you that drug addiction is my means of support. I'm a recovery instructor in the very program that graduated me. The shine I lost is returning. At fifty-three years young, I might amount to something.

We were stunned when Lamar was found dead in his apartment, discovered by another member of the UMD staff. He had been a support and source of inspiration for many of the UMD clients.

LIFE STORY AS TESTIMONY

In any cultural setting, there is a variety of narrative plots available to use as interpretive lenses to make sense of life. In addition to the plot of the addiction story, I have heard the "tough guy survivor" plot, wherein a man goes to prison for committing big-time crimes and survives incarceration tougher than ever. I also heard "war story" plots while I worked in the women's prison, in which women tell stories of how tough they are and what crimes they have gotten away with. These available plots, and there are more, are "culturally available models for self-construction."[5]

The stories I have heard that bore marks of church testimony run counter to the stories told about them by the dominant culture. These narrators command the floor and tell their own story, rejecting the larger culture's demeaning and inaccurate stories. They confront the "danger" of having "a single story" by countering the dominant story told about them with their own stories.[6] Among a limited number of plots in any social setting, the people I met in the Prayer Service most often chose "testimony" as the plot for constructing the story they tell me and the self they reveal to me.

---

5. Mary Jo Maynes, Jennifer L. Pierce, and Barbara Laslett, *Telling Stories: The Use of Personal Narratives in the Social Sciences and History* (Ithaca, NY: Cornell University Press, 2008), 132.

6. Chimamanda Ngozi Adichie, "The Danger of a Single Story," filmed July 2009 in Oxford, UK, TEDGlobal video, 18:34, https://tinyurl.com/t839ceb.

The stories shared by the people I interviewed were often offered for altruistic purposes, to "help somebody." "I'll do it [tell my story] if my story can help somebody." One woman said, "I just hope people get hold to your book and somebody that's hurting knows that other people have been through some of the things that they've gone through, and it does get better. If you keep your faith, you keep your mind on God, he will move it." The narrators recognize that their stories have value as a means of sustaining another person, possibly offering hope, guidance, or warning. According to Chanequa Walker Barnes, "Using one's wounds as a catalyst for one's healing ministry to others is the hallmark of personal testimony, one of the most cherished historic practices of African-American Christians."[7] Many of the people I interviewed gave their stories as a form of testimony. They were aware that their stories could benefit others.

The stories below are written in first person using only the narrator's words, but they also inevitably bear marks of my own biases, purposes, and interpretations. The interviews were set up with the introduction that I am writing a book for pastors to help them care for people going through hard times, thus putting their storytelling in the realm of faith and using it for the purpose of edification. They are products of questions I composed, I have rearranged the pieces in chronological order, and I removed parts that I judged to be inessential to their story in the space a book chapter allows. I made decisions about the sequence, the edits, and the omissions, which will all reflect my biases and blind spots. Of course, the speakers also made decisions in the telling as they engaged in a generative, interpretive act of constructing their story. They do not deliver static stories that they composed in the past, as though presenting the hardened fruits of past creative activity. Rather, these tellings are a creative action in the present, and like all personal stories, they are products of an intersubjective encounter between speaker and listener. It matters who the hearer of the story is. The life stories I present are inevitably coconstructed by the teller and the listener.[8] They are dynamic,

---

7. Chanequa Walker Barnes, *Too Heavy a Yoke: Black Women and the Burden of Strength* (Eugene, OR: Cascade, 2014), 166.
8. See Maynes, Pierce, and Laslett, "Personal Narrative Research as Intersubjective Encounter," in *Telling Stories*, 98–125.

fluid, and arise in the context of a conversation between a speaker and a listener.[9]

Joyce had come to the Prayer Service several times, entering slowly with her walker, breathing heavily. I was drawn to interview her because she had told us that "God allows me to see his hand move," and I wanted to hear more about that. She told me, "It's been a gift that I've had for some time, so I don't blow my horn about it. I'm not better than, or you know, none of that; it's just that *my mouth happens to be a gift that God uses*. I can't help that. He gave me the mouth, so *I gotta say what he tells me to say*." Already the contours of a counternarrative begin to emerge. She establishes her authority to speak by virtue of a gift that God gives her.

Here is Joyce's story in her own words:

Joyce

I thank God because he gave me two intelligent parents. They didn't use it for nothing. An alcoholic and a cocaine junkie. [If they had stayed together,] that would have been a catastrophe. I can see that now, though, but back then, it was like my mother don't love me.

I got baptized when I was twelve. But I didn't know who God was. I didn't know what was going on. I went to church every Sunday, got dressed up. I got on the usher board, got on the little chorus, and just did my little church thing. I got pregnant with my oldest daughter when I was nineteen. Me and her father wasn't married. I went to my church to have my baby baptized. They wouldn't do it because she was out of wedlock. So I turned right around. Never went back to church. Never. I'm not going to your church if you can't christen my baby.

I had started getting into drugs. Here, again, coming into my mind right now, this meaning, God allowed me to see that if I stayed in New York, Imma kill myself with drugs. It was me hanging out with people. It's like, you're hanging out with your friends, then all of a sudden, they disappear and you're by yourself. Why

9. Jennifer R Wolgemuth summarizes my point: "The selves in narrative interviews (even past selves) are contemporary (re)constructions, are actively constructed and performed in the process of narrating, are limited and enabled by the available linguistic resources, and are co-constructed in the interview (or other data collection) context." Wolgemuth, "Analyzing for Critical Resistance in Narrative Research," *Qualitative Research* 14, no. 5 (2014): 588.

are they disappearing? My friend said, "Uh, look, truth is, they using." I said, "Look, let's go up to the pipe shop." Bought a brand new pipe. Bought a brand new bag. Bought a fifty-dollar bag of dope. He showed me how to cook it down from powder to crack. He showed me how to put it in the stem. He showed me how to smoke it.

[After] I started using drugs in New York, I saw that I was about to go buck wild. So I left New York and came here [Raleigh] for another life. And I did real good for five years. Really good. I had money saved.

The house I lived at [in Raleigh] was so raggedy. You could look through the floorboards and see the dirt and the ground up under the house. Right next door to the house was a little itty-bitty Pentecostal church. And the kids went over there one night, and they kept going. "Mommy, can we go to church?" And I know they kept going. They were saying prayers for me; I know they were. My grandma was praying for me, and just . . . we moved out of there. . . . [teary] They loved me this much. I was in a place where I didn't care. I didn't love me. I had a man who beat me like I was his child or his dog. My brother came from New York and got him a gun and came to my house after one of the episodes where the boy beat me, and he said, "I'll tell you right now. That's my sister. Don't put your hands on her no more, man. I'm just letting you know." And we weren't even raised together; it was never a thing with me and him being tight, but he wasn't having that.

So I moved on into the projects, and I moved to Marshall Court, which is a subsidized apartment complex–real good. Three bedrooms, formal dining room, nice beautiful apartment. Beautiful apartment. I met my first husband [there], and I married him, and my grandmother and my aunt kept telling me, "Joyce, don't marry that man; that man ain't no good for you. Joyce, don't."

Baptism

My daughter's little boyfriend's mom, me and her had been hanging out at the liquor houses–smoking a little weed and drinking liquor. She was at my house; I had just got off work. She said, "Joyce, I got a bag of that good stuff. Let's go get us a bottle, and you come on over to my house, and we leave the kids, you know." So I'm like, "That sounds like a plan." At that point in time, the minister came to my door and knocked. He said, "Your husband is willing to come to my church and get baptized tonight. Would you like to come with him?" So I said, "Yeah, sure, no problem." And I went on back in the house and kept on [talking about] how we was going to smoke this weed, and we'll be at the liquor house, and we'll be dancing.

He [God] had a whole different plan. So I'm like, "Yeah, OK, sure." So we went down there [to the church], and they had the little white dress for me, and go wade in the water, and they baptized my husband first; they baptized me second.

Chaplain, I will never, ever, ever, ever have that same feeling again. It scared me a little bit. When I came up, something left me, and something jumped in just like that. Like, I could feel it leaving my body. I was born again. I was truly born again. My old self jumped out while my new self was jumping in at the same time; it was like a pull. I've never experienced that ever, ever again. And it's like, oh my God, I can't believe this. I actually felt my physical self leaving my body and my born-again self coming in.

[After the baptism,] I didn't want to hear it, I didn't want to see it if it wasn't about the Lord. I kept praying for God to give me the knowledge and the wisdom and the understanding of his word, and he filled me quickly. He filled me quick.

And I'm embarrassed to say I didn't do anything with it, because I was supposed to. But then I'm also thinking while I look at it now, "This is all according to his time span for me." That was the time when I needed to get that. This is the time where I need that so I can give it to somebody else. And he's the only man I know. No matter what I do, he take me back. [*The minister?*] No, I mean that God! The only man. He'll be my father, my brother, my cousin, my uncle, my son, my nephew–he's all that.

Work

I've done some of everything. I've done retail. I've done cashier. I've done stock. My major job, my major profession was nursing. I took care of Alzheimer's patients and I loved it. I loved it. I loved it. I loved it. The best job I had doing that was at Spring Valley Village in Raleigh in the health center. It was for nursing care. I was a nursing assistant. I took care of the patients: changed; turned; make sure they eat breakfast, lunch, dinner, like that. I just liked to take care of the old people. Just the conversations, things that they tell you about their past–I liked to hear their stories. Loved to hear their stories. And I had a good rapport with most of my families because I took care of them like they belonged to me. I didn't leave nobody wet. I didn't, you know, I took care of them like they belonged to me.

Father's Death

I really couldn't say [why I started using drugs]. I think it might have been after my father committed suicide. It could have been loneliness. I was still mad at him about that. I took my son, only three years ago, to where he committed suicide, shot himself in the head. Like, right in the door of the house he just bought.

He tried to kill himself seven or eight times for my mom, and it never worked–for my mom because she left him. Just, he was so depressed. Then he was an alcoholic, and he felt that he was the reason mama turned into a bad girl. God has showed me what I could have done, what I could have turned into, and how he kept me strong during the times that would make me turn into that [suicidal]. Thirty-three years ago, he shot himself in the head. They claim that suicidal is in my blood.

So he hates himself because she became an addict. But when she died, she was getting better. I think God was about to use her for something miraculous, and Satan just came and snatched her away–because she was the executive secretary of the Bureau of Child Welfare in Brooklyn. And this man that she was living with punched her so hard, she slid across the floor and hit her head on the baseboard of the floor. And the next morning, she went to work and started having seizures and fell down at work. That was after she stopped using drugs. She might have still been snorting powder, but she wasn't "out there out there."

Second Husband

I met my husband when he first moved to North Carolina. I met him in the streets. It was during the time when I was selling my body, getting high. He actually paid for sex the first time we got together. After about the third time, I was like, "You're money's no good." He's like, "What you mean my money ain't no good?" I actually fell in love with him in the streets. And he was there for me all through my addiction. He never gave me money for drugs. But he didn't say anything if I did them. He made sure that I took care of my grandmother and my grandson. He made sure my rent was paid. Then he fell on hard times, and he started using. Thank God it wasn't to the level of my first husband. And since he stopped, it's gotten better. We went through a rough patch for a minute, but we dated for eighteen years, and we've been married for seven.

Getting to UMD

I was chronically homeless for years, [in and out of shelters]. [One night, the Raleigh Rescue Mission staff person said,] "Well you have to go now because I got a woman coming in, and she got seven kids."

So that Sunday night was my last night, and everybody kept saying, "Joyce, what you gonna do?" I said, "Man, look. I don't know what I'm gonna do. I'm waiting on God." I got so tired of that question. I said,

Well, with my good, good mind, only thing I can think about doing is getting me forty ounce of beer, sitting in Moore Square park, spill a little bit on my clothes, drink the forty ounce, go up to the police car, say, "I need to go to Hill Transitions." They'll take me to Hill Transitions. I go in there in their detox, and I tell them I smoked $1,000 worth of crack last night, and I'm still drinking, and I want another hit–I need help. They will automatically put me in their detox. From the detox, I go to the overnight shelter. From the overnight shelter, I go to their program. By the time I get to the program part, I can go back to the Raleigh Rescue Mission.

But God didn't want me to go back to the Raleigh Rescue Mission. He didn't want me there. He wanted me where I can grow. And I can't grow in there.

I said, "I'm just waiting on God." She [Raleigh Rescue Mission staff person] said, "Well, you know, if you go on a Monday, you could go to Durham Urban Ministry, and you could get a bed." Here again, [I'm] small minded.

God promise our minds so much. He allows us to see just a little bit, just a little bit at a time. And I think he does that for me, for encouragement–because I don't have anybody to encourage me. So I have to encourage myself. So a lot of times, he seem to be [showing me] just little, itty-bitty stuff. And it's like, God's still got me. And I told her that. I said, "Well, I'm just gonna wait on God, baby."

At that time, at that point, the sky opened up. Flood rains. I said, "Baby, that sounds good. I got no way to get to Durham." She said, "Yes, you do." She reached in her pocket. She pulled out a regional day pass and a data day pass. She said, "You can get to Durham now." But guess what's even so remarkable about that?

The Durham bus sat in the bus station for twenty minutes while her and I was talking. And when we finished, and she gave me the pass, it was still sitting there until I walked on down and got on it. Chaplain, let me tell you. God brought me here. God brought me to this place—because this is where the second half of my growing is taking place.

I was at the point where I couldn't get a bed anywhere. So I came. Pouring down rain; soaking wet, wet like a little wet dog; water hanging off the dreads.

When I got here, I had that little metal walker; I had a big bag in the middle, right here, on that side. I had a suitcase, a pulling suitcase, with a handle attached here, and I was struggling. But I made my way on that here, and when I got . . . everything happens for a reason. Every time I recount to somebody, I can see where his hand was in that. Every time I tell the story, I can see his hand.

First Days at UMD

I've been on that same bed in the big dorm since they moved me in there. I have been sick. I've gone to the hospital. I've got where I can hardly move around; they allow me to lay in the bed. They brought me dinner, the whole nine. You know what I'm saying? I mean, God took care of me right there where I was.

So my first blessing was getting to Durham. My second blessing was getting in Urban Ministries. My third blessing . . . the man walked up to me, did not know me from a can of paint, he said, "Miss, I've been watching you struggle all week. You need a walker." I said, "Yes, sir. I really do." He said, "You know what? I'm going to the VA [Veterans Administration] on Monday. I'm gonna bring you back a walker." So God gave me this [walker], because he put in that man's heart to do that for me. You know what I'm saying? He knows what I need when I need it, and I just love when he allows me to see that. Why didn't I see it right there when it was happening? But thank you for letting me see it now.

A pastor I had a long time ago [said], "When you're reading your Bible, put yourself in the text and see what God is telling you. You can find out what he's telling you by putting yourself in the text." And that's what I did in Isaiah. I put myself in the text. I'm like, "Wow, this is really me"—'cause these are the things I'm going through. It's not a particular thing, but these feelings and emotions, it's what I'm going through.

Security Guard Incident

[A few days ago,] I woke up. And I was dry heaving and running off at the same time. And my heart was doing like this [*gesticulating with her hand*]. They kept me [at the hospital] for I think three days. About three days. And they let me go. God allows me to see his hand move. And it's been a gift that I've had for some time, so I don't blow horn about it. It's just that my mouth happens to be a gift that God uses. I can't help that. He gave me the mouth, so I gotta say what he tells me to say.

I had an incident with a security guard. He came down the hall and said, "Man in the hall." I said, "Are you a real man, for real?" And he said I disrespected him, and he gave me a twenty-four [*leave the shelter for twenty-four hours*]. He said, "You got five minutes to get your stuff together, and if you don't have it together in five minutes, I'll have the police escort you off." So three Durham police officers came. One day after I got out the hospital, I'm walking with a walker. A big book bag on here with my clothes in it. They escorted me out. I asked the police, I said, "Well, can I sit right here on the porch? Because my husband's on his way back from a job interview."

Police officer . . . really didn't want to bother me. [But] the [security guard] looked back at him, and he says, "I want her off property."

Yeah, he [security guard] came and kicked me out. And it's so weird because it's like, Lord, what is really, really, really going on? Now I'm scared. I'm scared. I know he's with me, but I'm scared. Because I don't know what I have to go through. See, when it's times like that, he doesn't reveal certain things to me, but when I look back, I can see where. You know? Because I love when he shows me how his hand moves. Especially in *my* life, it's just so awesome.

So I started crying. My first thought was "Get to Raleigh, to my older daughter's house. Wash some clothes. OK, you good 'cause you wanted to spend some time with the babies anyway. So twenty-four hours, you go back tomorrow, and you'll be all right. You'll be calmed down." But in the back of my mind, crack was on my mind–in the back recesses where I didn't see it. I couldn't go that far back. But God did. That's the amazing thing. God saw it. I didn't see it, but he saw it. So he allowed a bunch of circumstances to happen to keep me away from that.

I'm sitting outside crying my eyes out. And I called my husband. He said, "Baby, I'm on the way there. Calm down. Don't get upset. I'm on the way there, baby." I said, "Well, baby, I, I, well, I gotta go to Raleigh." He said, "No, you're not going to Raleigh and leaving me here. And both of us with our addictions, where I'm at right now, I'm in a good place."

So I'm waiting on him, and before the bus came [I thought], "Dummy, you got money in the bank!" Like, wow. I forgot about that money I put in the bank. "OK, honey. Let's go to the bank. Let's take out some money, get us a room, and stay all night." And then . . . he had to come back and get him a twenty-four so he could be out the same time I was out. OK, so he did that. [We got a hotel room and] we smoked cigarettes, we laughed and talked, we drank soda, we had a good time. It was "me" time that we needed.

Anyway. God saw that too. He saw that we needed to just have a husband and wife moment. Yeah, so . . . I'm looking at him; I'm like, "OK, God. I got money out the bank, and I'm sitting at the table eating. And he's sitting on the bed." And I'm like, "Get thee behind me, Satan." He said, "Baby, what you talking about?" I said, "Nothing." I wait about twenty, thirty minutes: "Get behind me, Satan!" He said, "Baby, what you talking about?" I said, "Nothing." I said it third. He said, "You will tell me what you talking about." I said, "Well, baby, you gotta realize I'm your codependent, and you're my codependent. The last time that we were in a hotel room and I was sitting at a table like this, I had food and crack and liquor on the table in front of me. And right now, I'm sitting here with just a pizza." And God saw that too.

What the enemy wanted me to do was spend up all my money on drugs. I was supposed to get my money, have a one-track mind, go right to Raleigh. And that would have ended up with both of us using. Both of us, both of us falling back. I actually could sit down and say, "Oh my God. Lord, I thank you. Because you just delivered me out that whole problem, and I didn't have to do anything but sit here." There's no sacrifice. I had to just sit here. All I had to do.

The day we came back, they gave me my mail from the day before. Had I still been on property [when I received my ATM card in the mail], I would have gone to the ATM machine, and what little bit of money I'd saved toward my housing here, I would have blown it [on drugs] in an instant. And I know I would. But that was God. He saw that was gonna happen.

Devotional Life

[I read] *Daily Bread*, inspirational books, the Bible itself, anything because hearing is the most important thing. You can look at the Word all day and all night, but the Bible tells you you have to hear the Word. And then when certain things come up, "Come on, baby. Pray." And when we're together, when we're outside together and we're separating or something's happening or I just feel the need, I just tell him to pray.

I just rely on God. Every morning before I leave out that dorm, I read the whole armor of God [Ephesians]. I put the whole armor on. Every morning. The sister that's here now told me about that. And I said, "Let me see if this is gonna work." And I do it. And I still get frustrated. I still get upset. I still wanna scream and shout at people about what they're doing wrong. But then I say, "OK, who am I?" I'm a trooper. And I know God's got me. It looks so dim, but I've been told by many ministers that when it looks that way, he's right there at your back. [*teary*] I have to count on that. I have to count on that. I have to count on that. Because looking at things, it's so bleak, I would give up. That's why I said, "I know God's got me."

Grandchildren

I look back at little different things that I've read online—documentaries; I love documentaries. I'm a geek. I'm really a geek. But I was watching something, and they were talking about children and how impressionable they are and different ways that you should or shouldn't raise them. OK, my youngest daughter tells me all the time, "Mom, quit telling Donna [granddaughter] that stuff, man, because you're going to build her up with that stuff, and when it don't happen, her whole world gonna fall apart." I said, "Wait a minute. Let me explain this to you." Every morning I'm with her, "Donna, you are so pretty today. You are so beautiful. You're my baby; you know what, Donna? God said you're beautifully, wonderfully made. You are so gorgeous. You are so gorgeous." And I say this to her every day. And [my daughter is] saying, "In reality, the world's not like that, Mom. You're setting her up for a fail." No. I'm setting her up for what God said she was. OK. And that don't go far from her.

And that [oldest] one, he's just so smart; I'll turn him into a geek. He turned on the TV, I said, "Find us a good movie. I found the last one; you find a good movie." He flipping and flipping and flipping—and flip real fast and don't say nothing. [He said,] "No, you know what?" I said, "What?" "I'm going back over here, back to the History channel because I think there's something I might need to learn." I got him. He's a World War II buff like me.

Just for the few nights the last time I stayed with them, just for the few nights that I was there, when I came back, he [the oldest one] said, "But, Nana." I said, "What?" "Nana, we gonna do the prayer thing again tonight?" I said, "Yes, sir." I make them sit right in front of me, all three of them. One at a time. One at a time. "I pray the Lord my soul to keep." Yes, and they got to remembering it. And then I say, "Who are you blessing now, come on; who you gonna say thank you to?" It's like, wow. "Nana, we gonna do that again?" I said, "We're gonna do it every night that I'm here. Every night that I'm here."

There are multiple ways this story could be interpreted: a story of God's intervention, a story of a "fallen woman" getting a second chance, or a story of manipulation of public services. I understand her account as a resistance story. This is manifest in three ways.

One, it is a resistance story because it recounts acts of the *subversion* of systems in order to obtain what she needs to survive. For example, the man who receives services from the VA acquired a brand-new walker for her—no doubt through deceptive means. In addition, her husband purposely broke rules in order to get "a twenty-four" so that he could spend the night in a hotel with his wife. The most complex subversion is displayed as an elaborate five-step plan to find shelter. When she was put out of the Raleigh Rescue Mission, she devised a complicated plan to acquire shelter until she could return.

> She would spill beer on her clothes and then finish the
>   bottle.
> She would approach the police and ask to be taken to a drug
>   detox facility.
> At this facility, she would lie and tell them she had smoked
> $1,000 worth of crack the night before, she is still
>   drinking, she wants another hit, and she needs help.
> She would stay in detox until she was moved to an overnight
>   shelter to participate in their recovery program.
> By that time, enough time will have elapsed, and she can
>   return to the Raleigh Rescue Mission.

While some might call this a story of exploitation and manipulation of public, private, and law enforcement services, it could also be a story of survival through the subversion of larger systems, over which she had no control. Through her ingenuity under oppressive circumstances, she would survive. She "creatively turned structures of power to her advantage" in order to survive as a disabled, unsheltered woman.[10]

Two, it is a resistance story because it tells a *counterstory* to the stories usually told about unhoused Black women who live with a substance use disorder and exchange sex for money. Facts emerge that run counter to the stereotype of an unemployed, lazy, passive, ignorant, promiscuous, impoverished Black woman. Christie Cozad Neuger says, "A counterstory is always a rebellious story— emerging when the counterstory is recognized to be more true than the dominant story and serving to resist the dominant story."[11] In critical race theory, "counterstorytelling" is both a "method" and a "tool."[12] As a *method*, it is "telling the story of those experiences that have not been told (i.e., those on the margins of society)." Joyce is telling a story from the margins that is rarely told, bringing nuances, corrections, contradictions, and additions to the story told about her in the dominant discourse. As a *tool*, it is used to "challenge the stories [told by] those in power and whose story is a

---

10. Antonio Eduardo Alonso, "Listening for the Cry: Certeau beyond Strategies and Tactics," *Modern Theology* 33, no. 3 (2017): 372. We see Michel de Certeau's notion of "tactics" displayed here. He contrasts strategies, "the seemingly totalizing plans of power structures and large institutions," with tactics, "the quotidian practices of those who appear to be dominated by strategies that creatively turn structures of power to their advantage." Alonso, 372. Alonso cites Michel de Certeau, *The Practice of Everyday Life*, trans. Steven F. Rendall (Berkeley: University of California Press, 1984), xiv.

11. Christie Cozad Neuger, *Counseling Women: A Narrative, Pastoral Approach* (Minneapolis: Fortress, 2001), 134.

12. Critical race theory emerged from legal studies and has influenced a broad spectrum of disciplines that seek to address race and power. According to Richard Delgado and Jean Stefancic, "The critical race theory (CRT) movement is a collection of activists and scholars engaged in studying and transforming the relationship among race, racism, and power. The movement considers many of the same issues that conventional civil rights and ethnic studies discourses take up but places them in a broader perspective that includes economics, history, setting, group and self-interest, and emotions and the unconscious." Delgado and Stefancic, *Critical Race Theory: An Introduction*, 3rd ed. (New York: New York University Press, 2017), 3. Barbara J. McClure also includes critical race theory, along with critical race feminist theory, to speak of counterstories in pastoral care and counseling. McClure, "The Social Construction of Emotions: A New Direction in the Pastoral Work of Healing," *Pastoral Psychology* 59, no. 6 (2010): 799–812.

natural part of the dominant discourse—the majoritarian story."[13] Her counterstory contradicts the stories told about her by the dominant discourse, and furthermore, this counterstory is told from the perspective of faith. According to Stephanie Mitchem, "Faith, for many black women, becomes a self-defining center that *resists socially constructed stereotypes*."[14] Telling her story in the language of faith is telling a resistance story.

She tells a counterstory to a particularly cruel story told about Black women with little to no income: the story of the "welfare queen," the woman who bears multiple children in order to increase the support she receives from the government.[15] In her story, she surfaces facts of her life that do not fit this cruel dominant image. In her case, she only has three children, and sexual behavior is not a means of avoiding work through childbearing and increasing government subsidies. Rather, some of her sexual behavior is work and a way to access the cash needed to support her children. This occupation provided the unexpected by-product of meeting her husband, with whom she fell in love and with whom she has been in a relationship for eighteen years. In fact, she never mentioned

---

13. Daniel G. Solórzano and Tara J. Yosso, "A Critical Race Counterstory of Race, Racism, and Affirmative Action," *Equity & Excellence in Education* 35, no. 2 (2002): 156. Solórzano and Yosso describe how critical race counterstories serve pedagogical ends, and the same could be said of how counterstories promote the emancipatory goals of liberation theology:

> Critical race counterstories can serve several pedagogical functions: (1) they can build community among those at the margins of society; (2) they can challenge the perceived wisdom of those at society's center; (3) they can open new windows into the reality of those at the margins of society by showing the possibilities beyond the ones they live and showing that they are not alone in their position; (4) they can teach others that by combining elements from both the story and the current reality, one can construct another world that is richer than either the story or the reality alone; and (5) they can provide a context to understand and transform established belief systems.

Solórzano and Yosso, 156. They cite Richard Delgado, "Storytelling for Oppositionists and Others: A Plea for Narrative," *Michigan Law Review* 87, no. 8 (1989): 2411; and Reneta Lawson, "Critical Race Theory as Praxis: A View from Outside to Outside," *Howard Law Journal* 38, no. 2 (1995): 353.

14. Mitchem, "Jesus Is My Doctor," 287 (emphasis mine).

15. Ronald Reagan spread the use of this derogatory phrase during his candidacy for president. See Josh Levin's *The Queen: The Forgotten Life behind an American Myth* (New York: Little, Brown, 2019).

receiving cash benefits from any governmental entity, though she did live in subsidized housing.

Contrary to many assumptions about people who live in poverty, she is not averse to work.[16] She had a variety of jobs, and furthermore, there were periods of employment that were very fulfilling, particularly when she was working as a nursing assistant ("I loved it. I loved it. I loved it."), where she paid close attention to her patients' comfort. Her husband also worked.

Her story challenges the image of a passive victim. She shows agency through her rejection of her family church, which refused to baptize her child, and she vowed never to return. She demonstrated agency in both her choice to use drugs and her choice not to use drugs by moving from New York to Raleigh. Her sex work as a means to survive can also be seen as an agentic strategy to survive.[17] Her ability to live in shelters instead of outside for two years required ingenuity and initiative as she maneuvered the nonprofit system of shelter. She chose not to go to Raleigh for the duration of her "twenty-four" because of the strong pull to use crack when she got there. Furthermore, the very act of calling upon God for help is an agentic act. It is an "active step" in the process of solving a problem.[18]

---

16. The following are Paul Ryan's words blaming the poor for their poverty: "We have got this tailspin of culture, in our inner cities in particular, of men not working and just generations of men not even thinking about working or learning the value and the culture of work, and so there is a real culture problem here that has to be dealt with." He was harshly criticized for his "dog whistle" racism in his referral to inner cities and for blaming the poor for their poverty. Wesley Lowary, "Paul Ryan, Poverty, Dog Whistles, and Electoral Politics," *Washington Post*, March 18, 2014, https://tinyurl.com/y56t9j7p.

17. Sex work is not devoid of agency. West says,

> *Some methods of coping and surviving may even have self-destructive dimensions.* . . . [Carey] also pointed out that 'selling her body on the street' at the age of twelve ended the sexual abuse by this man who was her mother's boyfriend. Carey developed these strategies to help her cope and survive in response to male assault. . . . *Certain resistance strategies have healthier effects than others,* but they are all integral to making even the possibility of healing viable. Our view of resistance must ensure that all its manifestations count. In the 'space' created by resistance, one is able to assert *a degree of self-control over one's circumstances.*

West, *Wounds of the Spirit: Black Women, Violence, and Resistance Ethics* (New York: New York University Press, 1999), 175 (emphasis mine).

18. Mitchem, "Jesus Is My Doctor," 287.

Other aspects of her story run counter to the majoritarian story. Both she and her husband had long periods of sobriety. They had family members who were professionally accomplished. She tended to her grandchildren's nurture and learning. She opened her home to relatives, and she valued her children growing up with an extended family. She was a "nerd" and a World War II history buff. She did not abandon her children, they and her grandchildren seem to be doing relatively well, and her daughter continues to participate in her life.

As she recounts the story to me, she asserts divine authorization of her words. She has an experience of special sight that was "coming into my mind right now" during our conversation. In this telling, she saw that her continued drug use would have killed her, and she took the initiative to improve her life and did so successfully for five years. This is not the image of the broken, desperate, urban drug user at the mercy of her addiction. This is an image of a woman who is confident that her words are validated by God. The *facts* she lifts up in her narrative form a counterstory to that told about her as a Black woman and homeless drug addict.

Three, her delivery of her story in testimony form offers an *interpretation* of her story that is also a form of resistance. She puts herself in a larger story of God's powerful acts, and constructing her story in this way is a form of resistance. If her counterstory above surfaces normally ignored *facts* of her life that run counter to the dominant narrative, this third form of resistance is an *interpretation* of her life that disputes popular interpretations. She calls upon a particular liturgical genre with its accompanying interpretive lens—testimony—for the telling of her story. This telling renders a hope-bearing, dignifying, vocation-affirming, and authority-granting account of her life. It is as though she seizes the pen or podium and tells her own story, rejecting the larger culture's demeaning and disempowering interpretations of her life. Even the very fact of her voicing her own story confirms her authority, humanity, and existence. She tells the story of a woman with a God-ordained purpose, with a God-sustained life, and whose God intervenes to provide a way to lead her to shelter. This choice to author her own life using a well-known communal ritual and literary structure—testimony—is a way to resist powers that both shame her and render her invisible.[19]

The words of a woman in a news program on National Public Radio echo the effect of giving one's testimony. In a news report on UNESCO's (United Nations Educational, Scientific and Cultural Organization's) declaration that reggae music would be added to its Intangible Cultural Heritage List, a Jamaican woman was interviewed. She reflected on the roots of reggae in the context of the hardship and poverty of her country, and this decision by UNESCO confirmed the legitimacy of both this music and the people who love it. She said joyfully, "We are real! We are real people!" In a similar way, giving one's testimony, and having it heard, is a way to say, "I am real."

The primary feature of testimony that appears in her words is honoring God for anything good that has happened. God had a plan for her to go to the Pentecostal church where she had a profound religious experience, and this plan overrode her own impulses to go out with her friend. Through her father's suicide, God showed her what could have happened to her because she has suicide "in her blood." When she was put out of the Raleigh Rescue Mission shelter, she said she was going to "wait on God," and then God provided a bus ticket and delayed the bus's departure. God "blessed" her by allowing her to be assigned a bed at Urban Ministries. God also provided a new walker. Through a complicated series of events involving a security guard and a missed

---

19. While her story bears many marks of church testimony, thus diverging from the story told by the dominant culture, she did not give a classic worship-based testimony. The most significant departure from the classic testimony form is the absence of a verbally affirming congregation that draws out and encourages the speaker to go on, to tell the truth, and that joins the testifier in praise and thanksgiving. Still, I provided an audience of one, and there was an audience of sorts that set up my invitation: pastors who read my book and care for people like her. A classical Black Church testimony might often begin with the formula "First, I give thanks and praise to my Lord and Savior Jesus Christ; he woke me up this morning in my right mind. He didn't have to but he did." Her testimony only partly bears the plot "I once was lost, but now I'm found." She does relay a remarkable experience of regeneration upon her baptism in the Pentecostal church, but she does not claim that it changed her behavior permanently. Her telling partially coincides with the plot "I used to be a hopeless sinner, but now I am saved from sin" when she says she did not know God before her religious experience but now she does.

ATM card in the mail, God saved her from using crack and gave her some time with her husband in a hotel. Through all of these actions, God is providing means of survival.

Testimony in a worship setting offers hope and reassurance to the congregation, which hears affirmations that "God is real," God is still at work delivering God's people. Testimony can also function as a form of self-talk that kindles hope and reassurance to the speaker. Her testimony that God is in control decenters the power of those who were depriving her of shelter. The Raleigh Rescue Mission staff person and the UMD security guard did not have the last word in her story. God did, and God was on her side. Their withdrawal of shelter was defeated by God's acts to provide shelter. The power of people diminishing her quality of life is relativized.

Her way of telling the story delivers hope. At several points, she reports seeing what God was doing only in retrospect. This indicates that there is a crack in the world's logic that loosens what seems to be a hopeless situation. Even when you are unaware of it, God is always there for you. God is working out something for you. You could be in the middle of a divine plan that is unfolding for your good and not know it yet. There is an open-endedness, an indeterminacy in life; it is not a closed cause-and-effect world because God is the one in control; ready to break the world's logic; ready to override impersonal, bureaucratic, rule-bound, unkind authorities.

She testifies that God is faithful and reliable. The one who is a provider will continue to provide for her. God is her father, husband, and brother. Under conditions of the fear of abandonment, this steadfast God will always be there for her. Under conditions of self-hatred, God will continue to choose her to speak to and care for. With the ever-present threat of violence, this God will persist in protecting her. The reassuring and encouraging effect of this testimony is immeasurable.

Her story also addresses the shame that is commonly an effect of trauma, and her life was full of trauma. Regarding her first marriage, she says, "I had a man who beat me like I was his child or his dog." She describes her father as an alcoholic and her mother as a cocaine junkie, and as a child, she felt as if her mother did not love her. Her father died by suicide. She lived in one shelter after another "for years." This testimony addresses shame through her claim not only that a divine power was providing for her but also that God was showing her things over and over. Her story changes the perspective: she is viewed as God views her, not as dirt, a prostitute, an addict, or as a lazy person. Her testimony subverts voices that say you are nothing, you are powerless, you have no one on your side, you are at the mercy of the world, and you are at the mercy of your own self-destructive impulses. Her story confers dignity and the identity of one who is tended to by none other than God, and her story addresses her history of trauma. Regina Shands Stoltzfus says, "Telling stories helps transform trauma. . . . Testimony is an important ritual in the process of healing. . . . [The] trauma story becomes a new story, a story no longer about shame and humiliation but about dignity and virtue."[20]

The story of her life that she told me is a resistance story in three ways. One, it is an account of her acts of *subversion* of power structures. Two, it includes *facts* of her life that are omitted in the dominant narrative and thus produces a *counterstory*. Three, it is a form of resistance as an *interpretation* of her life through the genre of testimony.

THE STORY OF A LIFE WITH A PURPOSE

I interviewed Darryl during a very stressful time in his life. He had recently been "banned" from UMD for a year, which means he was not allowed on the property for food, shelter, or clothing. In my experience, a sanction this severe is only after very threatening behavior or repeated rule infractions. He went through periods of regular attendance at the Prayer Service. He almost always had a testimony or a word of encouragement, and occasionally, he would sing with eyes closed in concentration. We thought of him as "one of ours," part of our "congregation." We were saddened that he would not be able to join us for some time.

---

20. Regina Shands Stoltzfus, "Couldn't Keep It to Myself: Testimony in the Black Church Tradition," *Vision: A Journal for Church and Theology* 10, no. 2 (2009): 47. Furthermore, "testimony has an easily detected *personal* dimension, a confessional aspect. Yet testimony also has a *public* dimension, as critique and naming of what needs to be corrected and changed." Stoltzfus, 47 (emphasis mine).

His circumstances were different from Joyce's. She was drug-free, meeting with a social worker to get housing, and on good terms with her husband, daughter, and grandchildren. Her circumstances were improving. In contrast, Darryl's life was deteriorating. After being banned from UMD, he had a brief period in a halfway house but then was asked to leave. At the time of my interview, he was living outside and sleeping on the lawn of the church adjacent to UMD property. During the day, I would see him there asleep or reading. One time, he flagged me down as I was driving past his place on the lawn, and he asked me if I knew of any anger management programs. He recognized his volatility was a problem and wanted to address it.

Darryl

What don't kill you makes you stronger. You have to go through to get to. So if you're going through something, [and] you get through it, it made you a better person. And so you gotta give thanks for all things, no matter what it is. Because he allowed it to happen, it can't be as terrible as I might think it is. And even when you turn your life over to God, all those things that you like the most, those are the things that God doesn't like. So all those things that you don't like, God is using that to better you. He's never gonna put more on me than I can take.

There's a lot of things I put myself in. And the thing about that, he loves me through that too. His grace is sufficient. Even though [I think] I know better, his grace is sufficient. He allows me to get beat with a lot of strikes because I don't go the way I'm supposed to go, but he still loves me. But I do have to pay for the consequences of my actions. I have to pay for that. I still give God praise in everything, in every matter–it doesn't matter.

I lost my wife two years ago, and someone said to me–which is the dumbest thing I think I ever heard–said, "She's in a better place." And I looked at this man like he was crazy. What you mean a better place? What better place than with me? But that was selfish of me. What better place than with the Lord? I just miss her so much, you know, and it hurts so bad that she is not there anymore. And I thank God for taking her 'cause she really loved the Lord.

I prayed last night, not knowing what the answer was gonna be. I was like, "Lord, give me somebody that I can minister to"– 'cause I know that my testimony could save a lot of lives. And I know that when God gets finished shaping me up and molding me into being the person that he would have me to be, I'm gonna change a lot of lives, a lot of lives. But right now, he's working on me. I guess when I go through enough and decide I'm gonna live for Christ and Christ alone, then I can move on.

Halfway House

I can move from this position because not too long ago, I was in a thirty-day house. And it was the best three weeks I had in my life. I was clean and sober, off drugs. I actually felt good inside and out. And I don't remember ever feeling good inside and out in my life, and I'm fifty years old. I never felt good. I always had a problem. But when I was there, I had no problem. It felt good to get up in the morning, spend my day doing what I was supposed to do, spend my evening doing what I was supposed to do, doing my chores. Everything just felt good. And I got kicked out for something that was so [insignificant]. It made no sense.

And ever since I left, I went right back in; like they said a dog will return to his vomit, I returned right back to my vomit. But I look at it as there's more lessons for me to learn here first before I can move on from here—that's it; that's it.

I want it [sobriety]. It's just hard, very hard right now. And I've been sleeping outside behind the building. They found my stuff and put it in a bag [and threw it away].

God Has a Purpose

Yes. If you think about it, how many people in this world going through the same thing I'm going through? Sleeping outside; it's a lot of people that sleep outside right now. Right now. And think about it, hearing my testimony, a lot of people can relate to it, you know? And when I get to where God is taking me to, it's gonna inspire somebody else to want to do the same thing. I'm gonna be an inspiration to somebody.

But also, I know this: that God had a purpose and a plan for my life. And I'm like Jonah. I ran from it. I ran from it. I didn't want to . . . not that I didn't want to do it—I wanted to do *me*. I want to do what Darryl like, you know? Not saying I don't want to do what God wants me to do, but I put Darryl before God. And so when I put Darryl before God, I gotta go through what I'm going through.

You know, Jonah had to get in the storm and got spit out in the ocean, got in the belly of a big fish. I'm pretty sure it wasn't the nicest place in there. But he had to go through that. He had to go through that to get to what God wanted him to do. I want my life to change lives. I want my life to be a book to somebody. I want to be a mentor to a lot of young adults, kids. You know, all the slinging guns and doing all kind of crazy stuff that, you know, you think you're grown.

Like my little nephew this weekend. This eleven-year-old boy told her [my mother] what he don't want to do. She said, "Get up." He got up and kicked the pillow on the floor and slammed his little blanket down and everything. I said, "If I would have did that, I would have been knocked out. Sleep on the floor." And I told him, "You know what? When she tell you to do something, you don't pay no bills, you don't do nothing here but eat, sleep, and do what you want to do. She tell you to do something, you get up and do it." 'Cause I let him know, "I'm fifty years old; you're eleven. You're gonna listen to what I say–period, or I'm dropping you, knocking you out. When I tell you to do something, you get up and you do it with your mouth shut."

He said something, and I gave him some words that, you know, some good ones that I can't speak about in this interview. I told him, I said, "Boy, I will hurt you. I will hurt you. First of all, that's my mother you were disrespecting. She told you to get up, you get up. Period." And he was mad at me for the way I talked to him, and he started crying and all that, right. I called him a punk. And maybe I shouldn't have said that, but that's my reaction to him crying. I just wanted to explain to him that you respect your elders.

Background

I don't come from this. I had a good upbringing. I'm not from the city, I'm from the suburbs, that's where the rich people live. I had the best of the best at times. When you're out there, you just want to go out on the streets and see what's happening instead of being a kid a little longer. I jumped off the porch.

I started hanging with my brother; my brother hung in the streets, OK? He was one year older than me. And something about the streets–the streets just adopted me. I could fight. I could hustle. I could rap. I could do all this kind of stuff that everybody else was doing out there, and I was better than most of them.

At fifteen, I was good at what I did. I grew up with LL Cool J. I was better than him at rapping–all that kind of stuff. I could hustle and sell drugs and all that better than most. And I got out there, and I got out there. And I found where women were, and I could have all of them if I wanted them. And I ended up catching a case [getting arrested] and going to prison. The first time I went to jail, I was about sixteen. When I went to prison, I was about eighteen, nineteen. But like I said, my early education was good; my later education was penitentiary education.

My mother [was a] drug addict and alcoholic. My father was abusive. He used to beat on my mother, even though I never met him. This is what I was told. I knew the next man she'd been with; he used to beat on her. I remember watching him beat my mother up. He beat up all the police that came to go pick him up to go to jail. I remember [him] beating twelve police up right in my house. I remember that. And my mother was an alcoholic. She smoked marijuana. She smoked crack after a while.

When I first came down here, I was at my mother's house, and my mother was talking to me about my situation. I had been in prison for a while. She said [to my sister], "Tamika, come on. Time to get ready for church." My sister was fifteen. She said, "I'm not going to church." And my mother didn't say nothing, kept on talking to me. About ten minutes later, she said, "Tamika, I said it was time to get ready for church." And my sister said it again: "I'm not going to church." And my mother continued talking to me. I look at my mother like she done lost her mind. Like, OK. So the third time, my mother said, "Tamika, stop playing with me. It's time to get ready for church." And before my sister could get it out her mouth that she wasn't going to church, my mother had knocked her out–boom, slid under the table. And she never had that conversation no more.

Prison

Well, first time I went to prison, it was like five years. And every day, I would go to the library and get a book. I could run through a book in a day, two days tops. And one day, I missed the library run, and I had nothing to read, and every cell got a Bible in it. I started reading the Bible. And I realized these people is crazier than any book I read in my life. I couldn't understand, but it was like these people actually were God's people, and they would not listen. He actually would deliver them all types of stuff and led them by fire and light and all this kind of stuff. Fed them from the sky, got them out of bondage–he do all this stuff, and they still would not do right. And I'm like, What's wrong with you people? And it's the same thing with me. How could I say what was wrong with them when he done so much for me, and I still ain't do right?

I've read the Bible over three times, cover to cover. You know, and it's funny, like, situations like I go to jail; I get closer to God.

It's like I have blinders on. I don't want to see nothing other than God. But here [outside of jail], it's hard to put the blinders on 'cause I got women here, I got money here, and I got problems here. And I got this, that, and the third here, you know? I could stay focused on God when I'm in jail.

I walked into this jail, and they had the Bible study in the morning right after breakfast. So I sat down with the Bible study, somebody asked me how I felt about something, and I actually broke it down to the lowest common denominator where a child could understand what I was saying. I could put it in everyday terms. And they like, "Why don't you start teaching some Bible studies one day?" And it got to the point where he [the teacher] would teach it, and he had less people attend the Bible study than I would. I had a lot more people. I even had people calling me pastor. And I'm like, "Don't call me pastor, brother. If you only knew who you was talking to, you wouldn't call me pastor." I realized that I had a calling.

Then one time, I was in the holding cell, and dudes was cutting up, acting a fool back there—you know, the holding cell before you go see the judge. And at the time, like I said, I got my blinders. It's all about God. And I told them, "Let's pray." And I prayed, and prayer changes things, doesn't it? It toned down everything that was going on in that cell. And this young boy asked me to pray with him separately. And I prayed with him.

About I'd say a month later, I got out. And I was going to see my old girlfriend, see where she was at. I was still in love with her even though she had moved on. And I walked through these projects in Winston-Salem. And—I'll never forget it—this young kid come running up on me like, "Yo, hey, pastor, pastor." I said, "Who?" He said, "Do you know you prayed for me that time in the holding cell? And I got out." He said, "Thank you." And I went, "Wow. Wow." And the funny thing about that is, everybody that was in there with me at the time gave me the title of pastor. I had done everything under the sun. Everything—everything except murder. Attempted murder, [but only] attempted. I've done things. I mean, I've done some terrible, horrible things.

Yeah. I've done some things; I mean, just living the crazy life, when you live that kind of life and you don't think—'cause you have to think before you act. Me? I act, and then I think, "Wow, I shouldn't have done that. I shouldn't have done that." [*What brought you through all those crazy times?*] Grace. Period. That's what brought me through was grace. Because I wasn't supposed to make it through. I wasn't supposed to make it through some stuff, you know? And one time, I heard bullets going past my head. I've been there. You know what I'm saying? I've been through some crazy stuff in my life and all that, you know? And I think the craziest part of it right now is sleeping outside in the snow. That's about the craziest, you know?

I've been in and out of prisons for over twenty-five years. Haven't been back. But it's a whole different situation [outside prison]: certain things that you could definitely not tolerate inside a prison that you have to tolerate here. Like, say somebody call you, excuse me language, but a faggot or something like that. That is fighting words off the gate, fight till the end right there in prison. And it took me a long time to realize it; the inside [is] not the outside. And it took me a long time to recognize that, and it caused me a lot more trouble. Because certain things [that] I refuse to tolerate out here caused me to go back to prison. Like, I'm older now, you know; a lot of times, I wish I didn't know nothing about the penitentiary 'cause the penitentiary actually really messed up the way I think sometimes.

Brick Incident

And like, even now, being I'm more mature, and I've got past the penitentiary part, sometimes I wish I was still in the penitentiary mood because some things happen to me that I would never tolerate. There was a guy who stabbed me about six months ago–said I owed him something, but I didn't owe him nothing. He stabbed me. And I couldn't believe he stabbed me, because I know this guy. He stabbed me in my chest. And I didn't realize I was stabbed, but I saw the knife on the ground when he did it. I said, "You stuck me?" I'm trying to feel it; I don't feel it leaking or nothing. Later on, I seen it.

But God gives us so many choices–you know, make your own choice, freedom of choice. About two o'clock in the morning, it pissed me off, and I went and found him. I went looking for him. And I know he slept outside, so I went and walked in all the little spots where homeless people sleep. And I walked around, and I walked around, and I walked around, and I walked around. He was asleep on the step. He looked at me like I was crazy. I went and found a brick, and I hit him in his head five times with that brick. And God had to really be in his light 'cause I tried to kill him. I really tried to kill him. I swung hard five times. Don't you know, an hour later, he was up running looking for me. And I'm grateful to God that he didn't allow this man to die.

But like I said, he [God] used those things. For his own reasons. He could take that bad thing and turn it into something so good–'cause even though we had that situation, we're the best of friends now. People like, "Didn't that dude stab you? Ain't that the dude you beat with a brick?" "Yeah, that's me. That's what I did." I said, "Well, he'll never think about coming against me again–bet you that. He might try you all, but he ain't gonna try me." And like I said, some people in your life for a reason; everybody in your life for a reason. And you know what? I think I'm teaching him the same thing: that this is not the penitentiary.

God Knew

It has to be predestined because God said this in the Bible: He said, "I knew you before your mother knew your father." He said, "I know the amount of hairs on your head." So if he knows this, he knows what's happening in your life. He know how many hairs on my head, he got to know what's happening in my life, OK? He had to know I was gonna meet this man, this man was gonna stab me, I was gonna beat him with a brick, we was gonna become friends, and I was going to help him with some stuff, he gonna help me with some stuff. He knew what he was doing, OK? He knew I was gonna sleep outside in the snow. He knew I was gonna have this interview. He knew all these things before it happened. So at the end, he said he's the author and the finisher of my faith. So just trying to get to the finish.

In his story, Darryl does display some *subversions* of the powers. He manages to sleep on the grass where he is technically not allowed to, he no doubt received a reprieve from prison misery through teaching the Bible study, and he was able to acquire reversals of some of the bans placed on him by UMD.

However, most of his counterinstitutional behavior was less a matter of savvy subversion and more a matter of impulsive, aggressive behavior. This is not skilled maneuvering around the powers; it is rather a personal characteristic that continually subverts his efforts to improve his life, as he acknowledges. We can speculate that his bursts of aggressive rage are the result of trauma in his childhood. He was in jail as a child of sixteen, his mother was an alcoholic and used crack, he heard stories of how his biological father beat his mother, and he witnessed another man beating her. This level of trauma as a child is enough to render him significantly vulnerable to multiple adult behavioral, health, mental health, and substance problems, including aggressiveness and impulsivity.[21] He speaks of his impulsivity, saying, "You have to think before you act. Me? I act, and then I think, 'Wow, I shouldn't have done that. I shouldn't have done that.'" Any reading of the material on the effects of adverse childhood experiences on brain development points to the likelihood that these experiences have led to his behavior problems.[22] Thus far from a savvy person who knows how to "work the system," he displays the effects of childhood trauma in his inability to manage his aggressiveness.

Darryl tells a *counterstory*; his story includes evidence that runs counter to the majoritarian story told about him. This might be said about him: "He is a violent drug addict, in and out of prison, and unable to control his impulses, and he should be locked up because he is a menace to society." This story told from the dominant perspective does not include many aspects of his past and desired future. It does not include his wonderment and pleasure that some have called him pastor. It does not include his desire for his life to have purpose, for him to be able to "change a lot of lives" when "God gets through with me." It does not include a picture of a man who wants to eventually be a mentor to kids. It does not include the fact that he thrives in the structure of a halfway house or even in prison. He observes, "I go to jail; I get closer to God."

A counterstory is not a story that glosses over highly problematic behavior, but it does include elements and perspectives that are omitted from the story told by dominant culture. There is much in his life that we might justifiably criticize, such as his use of the word "faggot," threatening to "hurt" his young nephew and calling him a "punk" when he cried, and beating a man in the head with a brick. What his counterstory does is complexify the story of a man whom we think we know through the majoritarian stories told about him. His identity cannot be reduced to his bad behavior. He has other

---

21. James A. Reavis et al., "Adverse Childhood Experiences and Adult Criminality: How Long Must We Live before We Possess Our Own Lives?," *Permanente Journal* 17, no. 2 (2013): 44–48.

22. Vincent J. Felitti et al., "Relationship of Childhood Abuse and Household Dysfunction to Many of the Leading Causes of Death in Adults: The Adverse Childhood Experiences (ACE) Study," *American Journal of Preventive Medicine* 14, no. 4 (1998): 245–58.

parts of his life that display the generous, the familial, the tragic, and the purposeful.

Darryl's *interpretation* of his life is also a form of resistance. In addition to subversion and counterstory, he interprets his life as serving a God-ordained purpose. Rather than a story that focuses on all that God has already done in the past, like Joyce's testimony, his counterstory is oriented toward his God-ordained purpose for his future, which is to "save a lot of lives."[23]

In order to tell his story, he mines a rich variety of sources for the interpretation of his life. The language he uses draws on popular sayings, traditional sayings, and Scripture to convey the meaning of his life. These sources function as authorities that confirm what he is claiming. Furthermore, this language draws him into the world that also speaks these languages. By quoting Scripture, using sayings and proverbs, he is grounding himself in the community where he learned them, which is likely family and church. He is drawing near to his forebears in his use of these languages.

He calls upon popular sayings:

> What don't kill you makes you stronger.
>
> Everybody in your life for a reason.[24]

He uses traditional proverbs:

> You have to go through to get to.
>
> He's never gonna put more on me than I can take.
>
> God had a purpose and a plan for my life.
>
> Prayer changes things.
>
> That's what brought me through was grace. (The language of "Amazing Grace.")

---

23. I have had informal conversations with colleagues about a liturgical or storytelling convention within Black churches that is a declaration of confidence that one's suffering will be transformed into a purposeful future in the service of others. To this point, these conversations have not surfaced a category for this kind of speech.

24. This is a version of "Everything happens for a reason."

And he uses multiple scriptural sources:

> And so you gotta give thanks for all things, no matter what it is. (Give God praise in everything [1 Thess 5:18])

> His grace is sufficient. (2 Cor 12:9)

> Jonah had to get in the storm and got spit out in the ocean, got in the belly of a big fish. (Jonah 1)

> [God] led them by fire and light. Fed them from the sky, got them out of bondage—he do all this stuff, and they still would not do right. (Exodus)

> God said this in the Bible: He said, "I knew you before your mother knew your father." He said, "I know the amount of hairs on your head." (Matt 10:30; Luke 12:7)

> He's the author and the finisher of my faith. (Heb 12:2)

During the interview, he is calling upon the repertoire of meanings available in his past and his environment to construct a story that encourages, dignifies, and humanizes him. He cobbles together a variety of sources to create an account of himself, a bricolage of elements available to him.[25]

The worth of this story goes well beyond the articulation of his goals for the future. This story is about the present; it is about the meaningfulness of his current suffering. He is transforming his present suffering by giving it meaning and purpose: my current suffering is not for naught, it is not useless, and it will bear fruit in the future. Suffering can be more easily borne if it has a purpose. He transforms his years of incarceration, his failure at the halfway house, his years of drug use, his ban from UMD grounds, and his

---

25. The idea of bricolage came from Fulkerson, *Places of Redemption*, 233. She quotes Kathryn Tanner: "As Tanner says, Christians are always making meaning in the fashion of the 'brocoleur'—'a creativity expressed through the modification and extension of materials already on the ground.'" Tanner, *Theories of Culture: A New Agenda for Theology* (Minneapolis: Augsburg Fortress, 1997), 66.

sleeping outside into the seeds of a good and useful future. Rather than the world being a place that promises only defeat, failure, and further suffering at the hands of cruel internal and external forces, his storytelling creates a world where his defeats and suffering are redeemed.

If Joyce's storytelling strategy for claiming dignity and authority was naming all the ways God had already been intimately involved in her life for her good, Darryl's strategy was naming all the ways God was at work in him to prepare him to fulfill God's good purposes in the future. One strategy looks back; the other looks forward. Yet both have the effect of conferring full humanity and hope. Joyce's testimonial falls within the tradition of testifying that happens in many churches. If I were to bring her story into the larger universe of Christian texts and practices, I would put it alongside the recitations of God's acts in Psalm 105, for example, and the eucharistic Great Prayer of Thanksgiving.

Darryl's strategy of looking forward with faith at all the redemptions that God will perform in his life is similar to hope-giving "future stories" that disclose a possible and desired future. In the course of our conversation, he is reaffirming and reconstructing a "functional future story" that is "inviting him to trust that continuing to live is worthwhile."[26] It is more akin to what in my tradition would be the affirmation of faith in our worship. During worship, the leader says words akin to "In the words of the Apostles' Creed, let us say what we believe." Darryl's story states what he believes, which is an expression of faith in what God will do in and through his life for the good. If our Sunday-morning practice is an affirmation of our belief in the historical truths of our tradition, he affirms the truth of the meaningfulness of his suffering. Ours is assent to doctrine that affirms our place in God's sacred story; his is an affirmation of God's certain, transformational power in his life.

In the telling of their stories, Joyce and Darryl incorporate many of the beliefs and practices I described above: about God's provisions, personified evil, gratitude, purpose, prayer, and Bible reading. They have constructed resistance stories. Joyce's emphasizes testimony and Darryl's emphasizes purpose. They relate moments

---

26. Andrew Lester, *Hope in Pastoral Care and Counseling* (Louisville, KY: Westminster John Knox, 1995), 125.

of *subversion* of larger systems of power. They tell *counterstories* that include humanizing, dignifying, and often-disregarded facts and perspectives that contrast with the stories told about them in the majority culture. They offer *interpretations* of their lives that place them in the larger story of God's gifts and purposes for humanity. Thus, far from being an inert account of their lives, these stories are performing the task of resisting larger structures and powers that would disempower, dehumanize, and degrade them. Furthermore, the faith they display is far from a simplistic, naive take on God's ways of being in the world. They skillfully create their accounts from the plots at hand and thereby establish their identities and God's immanent power apart from the crushing environment in which they are trying to survive.

Speaking theologically, these resistance stories contribute to our understanding of God and God's ways in the world. The harmful principalities and powers become clearer as we hear the stories of people who have borne their brunt. These narrators know the contours of an economic system that created extraordinary inequalities and that chews up the poor and spews them from public view. They know more about evil than many of us because they have borne the brunt of evil's destructiveness. They also know more than most about the truth that nothing "will be able to separate us from the love of God in Christ Jesus our Lord" (Rom 8:39). These life stories relay knowledge of God that is less available to people who have never lived in extreme poverty. These survivors of extraordinary trauma can witness to the power of God with great authority. Who but someone who has been in the bondage of a substance use disorder and is now living sober knows more about the redeeming love of God? One who has survived intact after decades of incarceration has a particular grasp of the depth of the sustaining power of God. The grasp of the divine in these stories extends beyond that of people who have not experienced the brunt of evil's power or the reach of the sustaining, redeeming power of God. Granting epistemological privilege to the oppressed means recognizing the limitations of theological truths that arise in the context of greater financial, emotional, and cultural resources and becoming open to the disclosures of God in oppressive circumstances such as poverty, incarceration, and homelessness.

Joyce and Darryl are actively interpreting themselves and the world and doing so in a way that enables survival, both emotionally and physically. They narrate their lives according to available theological scripts. These scripts compete with other available scripts from the streets, popular media, and historical racism. Survival is the "good" accomplished by these scripts: the construal of self as Godworthy, the world as open to God events, and their futures as open to the movements of God.

CHAPTER 5

THEOLOGY IN PROXIMITY
TO THE MARGINS

IDOLATRY

The religious worlds I have described are maintained in the context of poverty, mass incarceration, inadequate social services, low wages, and lack of affordable housing. These injustices are manifestations of our great national idolatries, our worship of the idols of white supremacy and neoliberal capitalism. In the presence of this life-negating, death-dealing idol worship, many who are marginalized persist in the practice of their faith, and their faith enables them to survive and resist. People living in poverty are not free from bondage to idolatry; the marginalized are not sinless, but they are undeniably the victims/survivors of particular forms of idolatry: white supremacy and neoliberalism.[1] All human beings share bondage to sin, but some of us are in bondage in a place of

---

1. I use "victims/survivors" to refer to people who have borne the brunt of neoliberal exploitation and cruelty. It expresses their victimization while not reducing them to passive objects. Traci West refers to women who have experienced intimate violence as "victim-survivors" as a way "to remind us of the dual status of women who have been both victimized by violent assault and have survived it. Black women are sometimes denied an opportunity to have their victimization recognized." West, *Wounds of the Spirit*, 5. I have linked the words *victim* and *survivor* by a slash instead of a dash to indicate an "and/or" relationship between the two designations, though I am hard pressed to refer to some who have experienced the destructive effects of extreme poverty as survivors.

relative social, economic, and political power and some in a place of extreme poverty and homelessness.

White supremacy—"a political, economic and cultural *system* in which whites overwhelmingly control power and material resources, conscious and unconscious ideas of white superiority and entitlement are widespread," and "white dominance and non-white subordination are daily reenacted across a broad array of institutions and social settings"—has all the characteristics of idolatry.[2] The *fervor* of the adherence to white supremacy is indicative of idols' demand for perfect allegiance.[3] The strength of *institutional intransigence* when challenged to address racist practices also betrays white supremacy as an idol. If the lure of the idol is the promise of freedom from the trials of precarious human existence and it is believed that the idol is indeed the source of salvation, we will protect it fervently and blindly swear loyalty to it. Idolatry also requires *self-deception*, the denial of any evidence that they cannot secure us from human vulnerability, and this is evident in the "refusals" of white supremacy: the refusal to recognize the depth and breadth of the pain of people of color, the refusal to hear their voices, and the refusal of any suggestion of responsibility for a system of white domination.[4]

White supremacy's refusals became evident in Durham recently. Many of us have been working on increasing quality affordable housing for people in Durham, and we have worked hard and for a long time. However, it has become apparent that many places in our public housing became dangerous, dilapidated homes for their residents while many of us were looking the other way. One housing complex was evacuated because of carbon monoxide poisoning,

---

2. Francis Lee Ansley, "Stirring the Ashes: Race, Class, and the Future of Civil Rights Scholarship," *Cornell Law Review* 74, no. 6 (1989): 1024, https://tinyurl.com/y4yqzdbr (emphasis mine).

3. I am indebted to Edward Farley for this development of the understanding of idolatry. Farley, *Ecclesial Man: A Social Phenomenology of Faith and Reality* (Philadelphia: Fortress, 1975); *Good and Evil: Interpreting a Human Condition* (Minneapolis: Augsburg Fortress, 1990). For another exploration, see Stephen Fowl, *Idolatry* (Waco, TX: Baylor University Press, 2019).

4. Andrea Gibbons, "The Five Refusals of White Supremacy," *American Journal of Economics and Sociology* 77, nos. 3–4 (May–September 2018): 729–55.

with about 280 families resettled in area hotels.[5] Ninety percent of these families are Black, and most are single mothers. In 2019, this public housing project received a rating of thirty out of one hundred by the Department of Housing and Urban Development— sixty out of one hundred is a failing grade.[6] Yet so many of us never looked squarely at our public housing and asked questions. For me, they hovered in my peripheral vision, never taking center stage. We tolerated hundreds of Black families living in unsafe circumstances, even those of us committed to quality housing for low-income, low-wealth families, and we tolerated it year after year. This is the sort of "refusal" involved in systemic racism, the sort of self-deception involved in idolatry.

The idol of white supremacy works hand in hand with the idols of wealth and capital that are promised in the religion of neoliberalism.[7] According to Clodovis Boff and George V. Pixley, "The theological status of [neoliberalism] today is precisely that of a vast idolatrous cult of the great god Capital, creator and father of so many lesser gods: money, the free market, and so on."[8] A 2004 Accra Confession from the General Council of the World Communion of Reformed Churches underscores the idolatry of neoliberalism: "[Neoliberal economic globalization] is an ideology that claims to be without alternative, demanding an *endless flow of sacrifices from the poor and creation*." Furthermore, it claims "that it can save the world through the creation of wealth and prosperity,

---

5. Virginia Bridges and Martha Quillan, "Missing Home: What Life Is like for Durham Residents Evacuated in Carbon Monoxide Crisis," *News and Observer*, January 30, 2020, https://tinyurl.com/y2gd746k.

6. *Inspection Summary Report (POA) for Inspection (642029)* (Washington, DC: Department of Housing and Urban Development, 2019), 1.

7. Luca Mavelli, "Neoliberalism as Religion: Sacralization of the Market and Post-truth Politics," *International Political Sociology* 14, no. 1 (2020): 57–76. Mavelli notes the proliferation of writers who have described the religious status of neoliberalism, "depictions of neoliberalism as a religion, system of belief, 'kind of faith' (Graeber and Piketty 2014), and 'theology disguised as social science' (Petrella, 2008, 127)." Mavelli, "Neoliberalism as Religion," 57, citing David Graeber and Thomas Piketty, "Soak the Rich," *Baffler*, July 2014, https://thebaffler.com/odds-and-ends/soak-the-rich; and Ivan Petrella, *Beyond Liberation Theology: A Polemic* (London: SCM, 2008).

8. Clodovis Boff and George V. Pixley, *The Bible, the Church, and the Poor*, trans. Paul Burns (Maryknoll, NY: Orbis, 1989), 144, quoted in De La Torre, "Interfaith Relations," 87.

claiming sovereignty over life and demanding total allegiance which amounts to *idolatry*."[9] The idolatry of neoliberalism demands that we discard human beings all over the world when they are no longer useful commodities as laborers or consumers. The evils of white supremacy and neoliberalism combine to create lethal conditions for people who live in conditions of extreme poverty in America.

Idolatry insists on the *rejection of the neighbor* as a cohuman being, as a cocreature who is also created in the image of God. Idols require sacrifices. Through vast numbers of murders from the time people of African descent were forced on ships to endure or expire on the Middle Passage and through slavery's extrajudicial executions and death by beating and body-breaking labor, our nation sacrificed Black bodies to idolatries of white supremacy and capitalism. The lynchings of thousands of Black people in America were carried out by "the priests and scribes of a sacred religious practice reinforcing and producing, structured by and structuring, a hidden yet powerful god-idol of whiteness."[10] We serve our idol of white supremacy through the extension of slavery and Jim Crow in the form of mass incarceration. We "identify 'enemies' of the idol [white supremacy] for the purpose of control and murder . . . [and] create vast demonic social systems that guarantee the security of the idol itself."[11] Our worship of the idol of wealth has created vast economic inequalities that strain Middle America and discard the poor as refuse.

Our idols *promise security from the trials and uncertainties of human existence*, and so we protect them from all challenges to their absolute authority. We believe it is the idols that will save us from our vulnerability as finite beings, thus we reject any scrutiny of their validity. We vigorously reject challenges to white power and domination because these are believed to save us from the threats of finite existence. Whiteness promises to save us from financial

---

9. The full statement is available here: "The Accra Confession," World Communion of Reformed Churches, 2004, https://wcrc.ch/accra/the-accra-confession.

10. Sims, 32. Angela D. Sims in *Lynched: The Power of Memory in a Culture of Terror* (Waco, TX: Baylor University Press, 2016) writes of the enduring power of the memory of lynchings as well as the reluctance to remember and speak of them. She writes of the courage required of people when they entered into the memory of a lynching that touched their lives.

11. Edward Farley, *Divine Empathy: A Theology of God* (Minneapolis: Augsburg Fortress, 1996), 66.

want by securing jobs and the accumulation of wealth, and it offers absolute truths that save us from uncertainty and ambiguity. Racist systems of the production of truth provide a sure and certain knowledge of who and what is good, beautiful, worthy, and trustworthy and who and what is not. Similarly, with absolute certainty, neoliberalism promises wealth and freedom from want to those who work hard in a society unburdened by taxes, regulations, unions, and the costs of social services. At the heart of white supremacy as an idol is the promise to secure us from "radical contingency," the promise that "human uncertainty, limitation, and contingency can be overcome" through absolute allegiance to whiteness.[12] Human existence is inevitably precarious and uncertain, and our idolatries of white supremacy and neoliberalism promise safety and security from precarious human existence.

The Religion of the Poor

After the Prayer Service, several of us encountered Charlene, whom we had not seen in a year or so. We shared the sad news that a woman frequently seen at Urban Ministries of Durham (UMD) had been missing for months. The police had listed her as a missing person, and there had been a false rumor that her body had been found in a dumpster at a nearby shopping center. Upon hearing this news for the first time, Charlene was stunned and upset. Like the rumor mill, she assumed this woman had met a violent end. Finally, she said, "God got control. I don't care what the devil say."

In response to the unexplained, unexpected disappearance of someone, and the assumption that she had died violently, she offered her theological reading of the situation: God is in control in spite of evil's deceptions. Upon hearing the same news, many in my faith circle might have called for gun control legislation or increasing the availability of beds for homeless women. Or we might have shaken our fists at the cruelty of human life or lamented the silence of God in the face of great suffering, especially under conditions of

---

12. Christopher M. Driscoll, *White Lies: Race and Uncertainty in the Twilight of American Religion* (New York: Routledge, 2016), 10.

extreme poverty. However, Charlene's response was to affirm God's overarching power and expose the impotence of evil. She did not talk about legislative action or changes in social policy; she did not talk about her internal emotional reaction. She immediately read the situation theologically with the assumption that God is greater than any evil that befell this woman.

Her affirmation that God is in control is more than a theological reading though. It is also a call to trust in God's goodness and power. There is the element of the imperative in it. It is not only a statement about the nature of God's control vis-à-vis human agency; it is also a call to hold on, be of good courage, because the victory is ultimately God's. It is not only a statement of truth or an assertion of belief in God, nor is it only an interpretive category that draws an event, person, or feeling into a larger narrative of the defeat of evil and the triumph of God, who is always on our side, and it is more than a change of perspective, or reframing. Rather, in its utterance, it is also an existential invitation to trust in God, refuse despair, affirm the ongoing presence of the good. In a similar manner, to say the devil is a liar is more than a statement. It is a rallying cry, a call to resist evil. It is meant to shore up defenses against all that is life killing. It is a naming, an unveiling, an unmasking of evil's claim to ultimacy. Narrative interpretations of the use of the devil as an interpretive category might say that this draws an event into a larger sacred story where God is triumphant over evil. While this is true, it misses the call for a decision or particular action implied in ascribing something to the devil. Charlene responds to the presence of violence with an affirmation of God's power and evil's impotence. This is an example of how the religion practiced in and around UMD offers hope, strength, and encouragement, how it enables resistance to evil.

In a nation in the thrall of idols, Charlene and others practice their religion. I have identified a specific collection of beliefs, genres of speech, and spiritual practices that include an orientation toward God as provider, the response of gratitude, the attribution of evil to the devil, a belief in a purpose for one's suffering, and prayer, Bible reading, music, and testimony. These elements are part of a larger formation that includes dispositions, memory, bodily habits and gestures, the senses, material objects, physical space, and forms of intersubjectivity. This form of religion engenders hope, trust, positive identity, persistence, and kindness, which are, for many people, *central to surviving a season of living without a home or in extreme poverty.*

Rather than relying on a functionalist view of religion, in which beliefs and practices are reduced to tools that produce some social or psychological good, I understand this religious formation as mediating the transcendent, disclosing the presence of the divine, participating in God's redeeming power. I call upon the notion of "redemptive alterations," the understanding that God's "presence" is marked by transformations in the direction of some good.[13] Such redemptive alterations might be the transformation of illness into health, the transformation of hatred into love, the transformation of a relationship of exploitation to one of mutual support, the transformation of a congregation from inward looking and self-serving to a place of welcoming the neighbor. In this case, I focus on a particular transformation: *the transformation of nonsurvival to survival* under conditions of extreme poverty or living without a home. It is this transformation, this mark of God's presence, that I want to highlight.

By survival, I mean psychological and emotional survival as well as physical survival, the enduring life of the body. The desire to continue living, and the strength to reach for what it takes to survive in the midst of humiliations, chronic stress, and trauma, are part of what it takes to survive. Ingenuity and persistence are required to physically survive under conditions of profound deprivation and violence. God is present in and through these religious forms that sustain the conviction that one's life is worth saving, that fortify persistence when it would be easier to give up. They offer hope for something good when it seems the only options are death dealing. They generate a sense of agency when feeling powerless. They form the basis of sustaining human connections. Feeling worth, persistence, hope, agency, and connections is required to emotionally and physically survive living without a home or in extreme poverty.

---

13. Fulkerson, *Places of Redemption*, 252. Farley, *Divine Empathy.* I put *presence* in quotes because as an adherent to the iconoclastic Reformed tradition, I am loathe to claim that God is ever fully present to human beings. We have glimpses, evidences, hints, but we never experience the full-blown presence of God.

We might be prone to imagining God's redemptive activity among people without homes to be limited to a departure from homelessness into a life with steady housing, employment, family, relationships, and church affiliation. This perspective emphasizes God's activity to heal, fix, and restore. Thanks be to God, this does happen. However, there are many times when a long life is lived with only intermittent stability or even chronic instability. Many times, God is present in ways that *do not fix* any external circumstances but that *enable people to survive* in the midst of difficult circumstances. People come and go from UMD for years, and some die in homelessness. While some people experience homelessness only once, many others are in and out of housing for years. Still others remain homeless for decades.[14] Yet they testify to God's presence with them. Thus rather than understanding God only as *the One who fixes*, I want to also speak of God as also *the One who enables survival*.[15]

If God's "presence" is only indicated by improvements, healings, and progress toward a physically, emotionally, and socially safe and satisfying life, then it would appear that God's activity is

---

14. For types of homelessness, see Barrett Lee, Kimberly A. Tyler, and James D. Wright, "The New Homelessness Revisited," *Annual Review of Sociology* 36 (August 2010): 503.

15. Survival is a locus of God's activity among many Black theologians. Womanist Delores Williams wrote of "survival/quality of life" as the form of God's work with Hagar, not full liberation. Williams, *Sisters in the Wilderness: The Challenge of Womanist God-Talk* (Maryknoll, NY: Orbis, 1993). Traci West speaks of "survival resistance" and claims that "when a woman survives, she accomplishes resistance." West, *Wounds of the Spirit*, 151, 165. Carol Ali Watkins also includes survival as a key sign of God's presence among Black women. Ali, *Survival and Liberation*. Gayraud Wilmore has written that Black religion serves the strategy of survival, along with elevation and liberation, strategies held in balance by Martin Luther King Jr. and Malcolm X. Wilmore, "Black Religion: Strategies of Survival, Elevation, and Liberation," *Journal of the Interdenominational Theological Center* 21, nos. 1–2 (Fall–Spring 1993–94): 145–64. Survival is also a political act: "The mere fact of black survival in a total system of dehumanization and exclusion is by itself a significant political act." Lincoln and Mamiya, *Black Church*, 201. This quote includes these citations: Wilmore, *Black Religion and Black Radicalism*, 15–39; and C. Eric. Lincoln, *Race, Religion, and the Continuing American Dilemma* (New York: Hill and Wang, 1984), 23–59. Homer Ashby claims straightforwardly that "to survive is to resist." *Our Home Is over Jordan*, 36. Ashby's claim can be read in two ways: "in order to survive one must resist" and "survival is a form of resistance." Both are relevant here.

quite thin for many who live under conditions of homelessness. If the only redemptions that count are climbing out of conditions of precariousness, or advancement toward health and wholeness, or reaching stability, then such transformations are absent for many who live without homes or who live for decades in extreme poverty. If God's redemptive actions are only in the form of a lifeboat and do not include staying afloat while remaining in the rough ocean waves, then God's salvific activity is scarce among many who are frequently or chronically homeless. Rescue, improvement, advancement are indeed transformations toward the good. They are indeed redemptive alterations. But transformation toward the good also includes the transformation of nonsurvival to survival. The religious forms, practices, and beliefs of the poor are ways God enables survival.

Simply to survive is a triumph over death-dealing forces. Missionary Richey and I were visiting a woman who had been taking meals at UMD. As we pulled up in front of her house, Missionary Richey noticed that her elementary school from over six decades earlier was just across the street. She faced the school, laughed, and said, "I'm still here!" Her declaration that she survived into her seventies was a form of both triumph and defiance. In the musical version of *The Color Purple*, the character Celie raised her voice in a song entitled "I'm Here," which not only declared her survival but also proclaimed the validity of her existence in the context of a world that had rendered her invisible and worthless. In the book, Celie says, "I'm pore, I'm black, and I may be ugly and can't cook. . . . But I'm here!"[16] To be able to claim "I'm here" is a form of resistance and defiance in a world indifferent, or even hostile, to your survival.[17] To be able to claim one's continued presence in the form of "I'm here" is not to be taken for granted in a world hostile to your very existence. To survive is to resist.

---

16. Alice Walker, *The Color Purple* (New York: Houghton Mifflin, 1982), 207.
17. The significance of "I'm here" was noted by Rev. Jimmie Hawkins in the Faith and Community class at First Presbyterian Church, Durham, NC, Sunday, July 22, 2019.

THE FAITH OF THE POOR AND
THE IDOLATRY OF THE RICH

Where will white churches stand in a nation in the thrall of great, destructive idolatry? We who benefit from white privilege have the urgent task of facing how we benefit from it, engaging in anti-racism efforts, and working with public efforts against social evil. We are called to address structural injustices in areas of housing, education, medical care, criminal justice, employment, food, and transportation. Some specific issues that demand our attention are changing how we ensure public safety, advocating for a livable wage, protecting unions, and making health care and housing a human right. Furthermore, the churches themselves are not above, outside, or beyond our social and economic context, as though we are somehow exempt from the sins and heresies of our historical location. Our national idolatries persist in our churches, and we know we cannot free ourselves through an act of iron will or super-human self-discipline. Freedom from bondage to sin is only possible through God.

In what ways does the religion of the poor and marginalized contribute to loosening us, ones who benefit from white supremacy and neoliberal capitalism, from our bondage to sin? More specifically, *can the privileged who are in bondage to white supremacy and neoliberal capitalism draw closer to the God who frees us from that bondage by drawing closer to the poor?* In keeping with my Reformed roots, I do not rule out any time or place or means for God's freeing acts to take place, but I do want to offer a perspective that the faith of the poor has elements intrinsic to our salvation from bondage to idolatry. This is not to say that yet another resource should be extracted from the poor, this time for the salvation of worshipers of white supremacy and neoliberal capitalism. It is not the job of the poor to save the rest of us. But it is to stand with all who claim "the margins of society are the privileged locus of God's revelation in history," and "we will not and cannot see or know that God unless we also make that our own privileged locus."[18] If God is the only

---

18. Roberto Goizueta, "Knowing the God of the Poor: The Preferential Option for the Poor," in *Opting for the Margins*, 145.

one who can break our bondage to sin, let us go to the margins where God is.

As I studied the religious faith of these victims/survivors of forms of idolatry, several themes rose to the top as keys for breaking our bondage to the idols of whiteness and neoliberal capitalism. I propose four spiritual habits for Protestant religious life, especially for my own Reformed tradition. It must be emphasized that this is not to romanticize the faith of the poor or their religious traditions; poverty can twist and deform even religious expression. Nor is this a claim that these traditions are infallible repositories of divine presence. It is a recognition that many who are poor have cultivated their faith in God in the absence of privilege on the basis of race and the access to wealth. What is the nature of this faith at its best, and how is it a resource for breaking our bondage to idolatry?

God will provide. Among people I know at UMD, God is trusted to provide when there are no apparent resources. This radical dependence on God is a refusal to deify that which is finite, that which is not God. It is a form of deep trust in the invisible God, and only God, because other resources are not at hand. It is only God who has been reliable in the past and is to be trusted to be reliable in the future. They live in a God-drenched world, where God is ever present to be called upon for survival. God gives guidance, stamina, moral fortitude, and any number of concrete gifts, such as a safe parking place for the night, a twenty-dollar bill, a bus held up in the rain. It is a world where God is *ever present* and *trustworthy.* Too many of us overthink God, what language to use, what makes sense rationally, what is OK to ask for. Too many of us confine God to sacred places or texts instead of seeing God as a constant companion who can be addressed at any time.

As privileged people deeply absorb from the poor the existential stance that God alone is the source of security, our bondage to idols weakens. We can learn from a faith that arises in a context where access to finite goods is greatly limited and where the only resource is the infinite God. Many of the people I know from the shelter have gone through seasons without access to any social, financial, or institutional resources of any sort. They are alienated from all family and friends; they have no money, housing, or public assistance; they have no connection to a church or any other institutions; they are utterly abandoned. The faith that grows from and persists in this context is one that knows that truly God, and only God, can save us. This deep knowledge of God, this way of understanding God as the only reliable presence, can loosen the grip of idolatry in white churches. With this trust, we will be more inclined to rely on resources less tied to whiteness in our forms of worship and music, interpersonal and deliberational styles, organizational structures, buildings and their adornment, and other habits and modes of life together as the body of Christ. With this trust, we will be less likely to protect the flow of income into our church budget, less inclined to hoard our financial resources, more inclined to freely offer our buildings and grounds to groups working for justice. We learn from the poor that trust that God will provide is not an impractical, otherworldly form of magical thinking. They witness to the reliability of God's provisions.

The devil. The category of "devil" does not require belief in a personal being who roams the world creating mayhem and destruction. The symbolic personification of evil in the form of demons or the devil or Satan offers a vivid, concrete, and focusing image that breaks through the refusal of white supremacy to see and hear the evil it renders. It also quickens resistance to the vast web of tentacles of neoliberalism that reaches far beyond economic systems and into psyches, intersubjectivities, and communities by throwing into relief the evils we confront. This category sharpens convictions, strengthens persistence, hones perceptions, and helps us see and name more clearly what we are all up against: "For we are not contending against flesh and blood, but against the principalities, against the powers, against the world rulers of this present darkness, against the spiritual hosts of wickedness in the heavenly places" (Eph 6:12 RSV). In this work, I see forms of violence and the desecration of the image of God in God's beloved creatures that point to the presence of demonic powers. To use the language of the demonic for this evil quickens my desire to resist evil.[19] It makes this overthinking, overanalyzing person move beyond the

---

19. Walter Wink wrote extensively on "the Powers" as a form of systemic evil that surpasses the material and operates in invisible realms. For example, Wink says, "Corporations and governments are 'creatures' whose sole purpose is to serve the general welfare. And when they refuse to do so, their spirituality becomes diseased. They become 'demonic.'" Wink, *The Powers That Be: Theology for a New Millennium* (New York: Doubleday, 1998), 5.

paralysis of seeing the ambiguities, uncertainties, and complexities of the situation. Some of us are easily detoured by the quest for the perfect analysis. But when suffering is attributed to the devil, the push is to risk acting even while lacking full knowledge, certainty, and explanation. The privileged would do well to name clearly the presence of evil—forces that destroy the spirits, minds, and bodies of God's children. When I first heard an adult refer to the works of the devil in the world, I was surprised. I did not know anyone actually believed that there is an entity called the devil alive and well in the world. However, I have come to understand the devil, Satan, evil spirits as ways to name what people sense as the world gone horribly wrong, a way to acknowledge that which we might want to deny. We privileged of the world have the luxury of living in denial of evil's reach and destruction in the world, the ability to ignore forces that create deep human suffering on massive scales. We want to deny it both because it is painful to ponder and because we are part of the problem. We want to preserve our dangerous naivete and false innocence, which disconnect us from gross human pain.

Gratitude. "I thank God for waking me up this morning." This formulaic opening to a moment of testimony acknowledges the graciousness of God upon which we depend for life itself. When I first heard this affirmation years ago, I thought simply surviving the night was a small matter for which to express gratitude. However, I now recognize in it the profound recognition of both precarious human existence and the necessity of God's grace for survival. The one uttering it recognizes both human vulnerability and God's gift of ongoing existence. It is not a given that any of us will survive the night, and people who have experienced homelessness know this better than most. We who are privileged are blinded to that fact by the illusions of permanence and safety that our relative social power offers. Habits of recognition of both the giftedness and the precariousness of creaturely life throw into relief the futility of idols of whiteness and neoliberal capitalism. To regularly recognize our dependence on God and nothing else diminishes our bondage to these idols.

Testimony. The deeply personal, sustaining, and transforming power of God is regularly given witness in my work at UMD. An instance in my church illustrates the contrast with my tradition.

The worship style in my progressive congregation is traditionally Presbyterian with occasional alternative elements, a form that I find beautiful and deeply grounding. One time during worship at my church, several formerly unhoused people spoke of an organization that provided them supportive housing services. Their words drew on testimonial form to speak of the impact of this organization on their lives. They spoke about God who provided for them when they needed it, about God who had turned their lives around when they were heading down the wrong path. They offered expressions of deep gratitude to God who had rescued them from homelessness. As they spoke, I was aware of the contrast with my church's more reserved and structured modes of expression. Their words were personal, vulnerable, and unabashedly God soaked. At another time in my life, I might have thought the theology was simplistic and anti-intellectual and the expressions uncomfortably self-revealing. However, on this day, I drank deeply of the divine grace they disclosed in their stories and was moved and edified. The spiritual habit of testimony as a way of narrating one's story grounds us in God's grace. Such a grounding is the only way to freedom from bondage to idolatry.

A Plea for Proximity

"There is power in proximity," says Bryan Stevenson, founder of the Equal Justice Initiative. He tells a graduating class "to get proximate to people who are suffering, to get closer to people who are excluded, to go into the parts of the community that other people say you shouldn't go."[20] In another setting, he said, "If you are willing to get closer to people who are suffering, you will find the power to change the world."[21] I might modify Stevenson's statement to read "If you are willing to get closer to people who are suffering,

---

20. Bryan Stevenson, commencement speech at Johns Hopkins University, May 24, 2018, available at https://tinyurl.com/y23789of.

21. Leondra Fernandez, "Empathy and Social Justice: The Power of Proximity in Improvement Science," *Carnegie Commons* (blog), April 21, 2016, https://tinyurl.com/y3ypz24f, quoting Bryan Stevenson at the 2016 Carnegie Foundation Summit on Improvement in Education.

you will find God who empowers you to stay in the struggle for the realm of God on earth." As mainline Protestants cast about for revitalization in the face of dwindling membership, the power offered in proximity to the poor is vital. I am calling for drawing close to people who are suffering from poverty, working three jobs, living in shrubbery, mumbling with a serious mental illness. In a way that is beyond explanation, in a way that is at the heart of God's option for the poor, I believe that as we draw near, get proximate, to people who are this world's castoffs, we draw near to God.

Our churches are faced with decisions about how much to challenge the idolatries of white supremacy and neoliberal capitalism. Some churches will choose the path of challenging these idols "even though the authorities and human laws might forbid them and punishment and suffering be the consequence."[22] As churches' confrontations with neoliberal powers draw us into ever riskier situations where sacrifices may be required, the spiritual habits we learn from victims/survivors of these powers will serve us well. To endure the cost of confronting the principalities and powers, we can be strengthened, encouraged, by the faith of the poor. Some people will make great sacrifices in job losses for speaking courageously; some will face humiliations, diminished income, discouragement, thanklessness, and defeats. The spiritual habits I have named will become more important to all of us as we confront powers that are crushing the earth and its inhabitants as the planet warms. I anticipate the need for a faithfulness that will be increasingly demanding as we proclaim a gospel alternative to salvation through whiteness and wealth. As the false god of white supremacy is exposed, people who have survived and thrived without it will be spiritual guides to the rest of us who seek to relinquish and dismantle it. As more and more of us engage in the ongoing effort to renounce neoliberal capitalism and white privilege, we will be sustained by the beliefs and practices of peoples who never had wealth or privilege by virtue of race. The poor are already resisting these powers as the ones who most obviously bear the brunt of them, and we have much to learn.

Churches respond to the problem of homelessness in different ways. Many churches respond by meeting immediate needs for a

---

22. Presbyterian Church (USA), "The Confession of Belhar," in *The Book of Confessions* (Louisville, KY: Westminster John Knox, 2017), sec. 10.9.

bus ticket, a sandwich, shoes for a new job, a copay for medication. Other churches provide referrals to public or nonprofit social services that can help with finding an apartment, a job, or health care. Still other churches engage in advocacy at local, state, and national levels, attempting to increase funding for housing and services or change public policy. A very few congregations welcome people without homes into the full membership of the church. However, I want to advocate for still another sort of space, one that is not owned or controlled by any single group. Similar to the Prayer Service, this other sort of group would meet outside a church building, and there would be differences of class, race, ability, sexuality, nationality, age, and medical and mental health, just as has been true in our Prayer Service. The participants would enter together into prayer, testimony, song, and Scripture reading. This would not be a perfect gathering; there would still be the problem of the "white ownership of space," elements of white entitlement, and self-protective Black "vigilance" and self-censorship.[23] But it would be where connections and conversions begin. It is through sustained participation in this sort of gathering where transformations happen. Through proximity, openness, absence of judgment, and mutual goodwill, "conversions to the neighbor" are possible.[24] I yearn for this sort of space to become more commonplace, for there to be places of shared vulnerability, gratitude, and praise.

~·~

It is not unusual for people to ask me what I have learned through my years working at UMD. Answers I have heard from others who have worked with people without homes include "I now realize homeless people are just people like me," or "I found such a depth of wisdom among the poor," or "I have learned so much about God's presence during difficult times," or "I received so much more than I gave." While these statements have some truth in them for me, I frame the learning, or the conversion, differently.

---

23. Fulkerson, *Places of Redemption*, 86. Fulkerson expresses her indebtedness to Dr. William Hart for introducing her to the notion of the white ownership of space.
24. Gustavo Gutierrez, *A Theology of Liberation: History, Politics, and Salvation*, rev. ed. (Maryknoll, NY: Orbis, 2004), 110.

I have grown in my understanding of the intransigence of poverty. When I started working at UMD, deep down, I held the unarticulated fantasy that anyone living in poverty could live simply but contentedly by finding a low-paying job, keeping up with the rent and daily expenses through frugality, becoming active in a church, and making a few friends, *or at least I could.* All that was needed was to stay out of trouble, forego luxury, and participate in a church. I knew about systemic racism, radical inequality, structures of injustice that kept people in poverty, but I whispered to myself that I would be able to escape the misery of poverty with my simple living and good values. Holding to this fantasy protected me from the truth that I live where I live and have what I have and wield the power that I do because of forms of privilege that have nothing to do with virtuous decisions and good behavior. This fantasy occludes white supremacist and economic structures that serve me and deprive the people I care for at UMD. Over time, I have been stripped of this falsehood.

The most important and sacred change has been an enlargement in the universe of people who may be recognized as a friend. There has been an increase in human shapes, colors, gaits, clothing, speech, and comportment that are familiar. They no longer immediately indicate "other," or someone I could not possibly know. Earlier, if I saw someone on the sidewalk in ill-fitting clothes with unkempt hair and a listless gait or the look of straining, searching, and uncertainty, I might have noticed them, but *I would not have thought, "There is someone I might know."* Now I look more closely and think, "Is that Mike? I hope his headache went away," or "I wonder if that is Sheila. I'll ask if her grandbaby was born yet," or "There's William. He got a new coat." There has been an expansion of bodies whom I recognize as familiar, or speaking theologically, as created in God's image. We may have shared a history, we may have occupied the same social space, and maybe we have prayed together. This change has happened simply because of where I have placed my body for three mornings a week for the last ten years. If earlier I was habituated to bodies that displayed the health and well-being typical of middle-class America, my habituations have been enlarged. This expansion of the universe of people who could be recognized as a friend is at the heart of the gospel that converts others into friends.

God called Abraham to leave all that is familiar and go to the land that God would show him. Jesus calls us to leave father and mother and follow him. These calls can be spiritualized, understood as invitations to a new self-understanding or an acceptance of God's grace or a new ministry. I have heard these familiar biblical stories as calls to draw closer to the poorest, most dislocated, most marginalized people of my city, believing that to draw nearer to them is to draw nearer to God. A very familiar Christmas carol addresses the ones who are "beneath life's crushing load, whose forms are bending low, who toil along the climbing way with painful steps and slow." They are beckoned to "look now for glad and golden hours come swiftly on the wing" and to "rest beside the weary road and hear the angels sing."[25] In my work as a chaplain at UMD, I have dwelled with people who are crushed and bending low, and we have rested together beside the road and heard the angels sing.

---

25. Edmund H. Sears, "It Came upon the Midnight Clear," in *Glory to God: The Presbyterian Hymnal*, ed. David Eicher (Louisville, KY: Westminster John Knox, 2013), hymn 123.

BIBLIOGRAPHY

Abingdon, Jimmie, arr. "If You Live Right, Heaven Belongs to You." In *African American Heritage Hymnal*, edited by Rev. Dr. Delores Carpenter and Rev. Nolan E. Williams Jr., hymn 582. Chicago: GIA, 2001.

Adichie, Chimamanda Ngozi. "The Danger of a Single Story." Filmed July 2009 in Oxford, UK. TEDGlobal video, 18:34. https://tinyurl.com/t839ceb.

Allen, Josephine A. V. "Poverty as a Form of Violence: A Structural Perspective." *Journal of Human Behavior in the Social Environment* 4, no. 2/3 (2001): 45–59.

Alonso, Antonio Eduardo. "Listening for the Cry: Certeau beyond Strategies and Tactics." *Modern Theology* 33, no. 3 (2017): 369–394.

Ammerman, Nancy T. "Finding Religion in Everyday Life." *Sociology of Religion* 75, no. 2 (June 2014): 189–207.

———. "Golden Rule Christianity: Lived Religion in the American Mainstream." In *Lived Religion in America: Toward a History of Practice*, edited by David D. Hall, 196–216. Princeton, NJ: Princeton University Press, 1997.

Anderson, Elijah. *Code of the Street: Decency, Violence, and the Moral Life of the Inner City*. New York: W. W. Norton, 1999.

Andrews, Dale P. *Practical Theology for Black Churches: Bridging Black Theology and African American Folk Religion*. Louisville, KY: Westminster John Knox, 2002.

Ansley, Francis Lee. "Stirring the Ashes: Race, Class, and the Future of Civil Rights Scholarship." *Cornell Law Review* 74, no. 6 (1989). https://tinyurl.com/y4yqzdbr.

Ashby, Homer. *Our Home Is over Jordan: A Black Pastoral Theology*. St. Louis: Chalice, 2003.

Barnes, Chanequa Walker. *Too Heavy a Yoke: Black Women and the Burden of Strength*. Eugene, OR: Cascade, 2014.

Baumgardner, Dawn Vaughn. "Durham in an 'Affordable Housing Crisis,' Council Members Say." *Durham Herald-Sun*, March 21, 2018. https://tinyurl.com/y2hwcl3d.

Bell, Catherine. "Ritual." In *The Blackwell Companion to the Study of Religion*, edited by Robert A. Segal, 397–411. London: Blackwell, 2006.

Biehl, João. *Vita: Life in a Zone of Social Abandonment*. Berkeley: University of California Press, 2013.

Black, Helen K. "Poverty and Prayer: Spiritual Narratives of Elderly African American Women." *Review of Religious Research* 40, no. 4 (June 1999): 359–374.

Boff, Clodovis, and George V. Pixley. *The Bible, the Church, and the Poor*. Translated by Paul Burns. Maryknoll, NY: Orbis, 1989.

Bridges, Virginia, and Martha Quillan. "Missing Home: What Life Is like for Durham Residents Evacuated in Carbon Monoxide Crisis." *News and Observer*, January 30, 2020. https://tinyurl.com/y2gd746k.

Brueggemann, Walter. *God, Neighbor, Empire: The Excess of Divine Fidelity and the Command of Common Good*. Waco, TX: Baylor University Press, 2016.

Bull City 150. "Uneven Ground." Home Owners Loan Corporation Map, 1939. https://tinyurl.com/y2uwknst.

Butler, Judith. *Precarious Life: The Powers of Mourning and Violence*. London: Verso, 2004.

Butler, Lee H., Jr. "Lynching: A Post-traumatic Stressor in a Protracted-Traumatic World." *Sacred Spaces: The e-Journal of the American Association of Pastoral Counselors* 4 (2012): 8.

———. "Testimony as Hope and Care." In *Living Stones in the Household of God*, edited by Linda Elaine Thomas, 24–32. Minneapolis: Augsburg Fortress, 2004.

Center for Poverty Research. "What Is 'Deep Poverty'?" University of California at Davis. Accessed February 9, 2018. https://poverty.ucdavis.edu/faq/what-deep-poverty.

Center on Budget and Policy Priorities. "Chart Book: Temporary Assistance for Needy Families." Accessed November 11, 2011. https://tinyurl.com/y2urbj38.

———. "North Carolina's TANF Cash Assistance Is Disappearing for Poor Families." Accessed November 11, 2018. https://tinyurl.com/y258rjsb.

City-Data. "Durham, North Carolina (NC) Poverty Rate Data—Information about Poor and Low Income Residents." Accessed August 9, 2019. https://tinyurl.com/y3sgaevu.

Cone, James H. *A Black Theology of Liberation*. Philadelphia: Lippincott, 1970.

———. *My Soul Looks Back*. Nashville: Abingdon, 1982.

Connolly, William E. *The Fragility of Things: Self-Organizing Processes, Neoliberal Fantasies, and Democratic Activism*. Durham, NC: Duke University Press, 2013.

Cooper-Lewter, Nicholas, and Henry H. Mitchell. *Soul Theology: The Heart of American Black Culture*. Nashville: HarperCollins, 1986.

Couture, Pamela. *Seeing Children, Seeing God: A Practical Theology of Children*. Nashville: Abingdon, 2000.

Cowlishaw, Gillian. "Race at Work: Reflecting on Fieldwork in the Northern Territory." *Journal of the Royal Anthropological Institute* 3, no. 4 (1997): 95–113.

Cresswell, Tim. *In Place / Out of Place: Geography, Ideology, and Transgression*. Minneapolis: University of Minnesota Press, 1996.

Curtis, Cynthia Ann. "Spiritualities of the Displaced: An Ethnographic Study of Homeless Lived Faith." PhD diss., Duke University School of Divinity, 2013.

Davis, Osha Gray. *Best of Enemies: Race and Redemption in the New South*. Chapel Hill: University of North Carolina Press, 2007.

Deaton, Angus. "The U.S. Can No Longer Hide from Its Deep Poverty Problem." *New York Times*, January 24, 2018. https://tinyurl.com/yafsq9vx.

de Certeau, Michel. *The Practice of Everyday Life*. Translated by Steven F. Rendall. Berkeley: University of California Press, 1984.

DeHart, Dana D. "Pathways to Prison: Impact of Victimization in the Lives of Incarcerated Women." *Violence against Women* 14, no. 12 (December 2008): 1362–1381.

De La Torre, Miguel. "Interfaith Relations and the Pursuit of Justice." *Review and Expositor* 114, no. 1 (2017): 81–89. https://doi.org/10.1177/0034637316687358.

———. *Reading the Bible from the Margins*. Maryknoll, NY: Orbis, 2002.

Delgado, Richard. "Storytelling for Oppositionists and Others: A Plea for Narrative." *Michigan Law Review* 87, no. 8 (1989): 2411–2441.

Delgado, Richard, and Jean Stefancic. *Critical Race Theory: An Introduction*. 3rd ed. New York: New York University Press, 2017.

Department of Housing and Urban Development. *Inspection Summary Report (POA) for Inspection (642029)*. Washington, DC: Department of Housing and Urban Development, 2019.

deRoon-Cassini, Terri A., Ed de St. Aubin, Abbey Valvano, James Hastings, and Patricia Horn. "Psychological Well-Being after Spinal Cord Injury: Perception of Loss and Meaning Making." *Rehabilitation Psychology* 54, no. 3 (2009): 306–314.

Dezutter, Jessie, Laura Dewitte, and Siebrecht Vanhooren. "Chronic Pain and Meaning in Life: Challenge and Change." In *Meanings of Pain*, edited by Simon van Rysewyk, 211–226. Cham, Switzerland: Springer, 2016.

Didenko, Eugenia, and Nicole Pankratz. "Substance Use: Pathways to Homelessness? Or a Way of Adapting to Street Life?" *Visions Journal* 4, no. 1 (2007): 9.

Doehring, Carrie. *The Practice of Pastoral Care: A Postmodern Approach.* Revised and expanded edition. Louisville, KY: Westminster John Knox, 2015.

Dolan, Karen, and Jody Carr. "The Poor Get Prison: The Alarming Spread of the Criminalization of Poverty." *Institute for Policy Studies*, March 18, 2015.

Downtown Durham, Inc. "State of Downtown Durham 2018." Accessed October 26, 2018. https://tinyurl.com/y2ffyjsk.

Driscoll, Christopher M. *White Lies: Race and Uncertainty in the Twilight of American Religion.* New York: Routledge, 2016.

Du Bois, W. E. B. "The Upbuilding of Black Durham: The Success of the Negroes and Their Value to a Tolerant and Helpful Southern City." *World's Work* 23 (January 1912): 334–338.

Dunlap, Susan J. *Caring Cultures: How Congregations Respond to the Sick.* Waco, TX: Baylor University Press, 2009.

Durham County Register of Deeds. Book 66, July 2, 1923.

Edelman, Peter. *Not a Crime to Be Poor: The Criminalization of Poverty in America.* New York: New Press, 2017.

Edin, Kathryn J., and H. Luke Shaeffer. *$2 a Day: Living on Almost Nothing in America.* Boston: Houghton Mifflin, 2015.

Emmons, Robert A., and Michael E. McCullough, eds. *The Psychology of Gratitude.* New York: Oxford University Press, 2004.

Farley, Edward. *Divine Empathy: A Theology of God.* Minneapolis: Augsburg Fortress, 1996.

———. *Ecclesial Man: A Social Phenomenology of Faith and Reality.* Philadelphia: Fortress, 1975.

———. *Good and Evil: Interpreting a Human Condition.* Minneapolis: Augsburg Fortress, 1990.

Farmer, Paul. "An Anthropology of Structural Violence." *Current Anthropology* 45, no. 3 (2004): 305–325. https://www.jstor.org/stable/10.1086/382250.

Farmer, Paul, and Barbara Rylko-Bauer. "Structural Violence, Poverty, and Social Suffering." In *The Oxford Handbook of the Social Science of Poverty*, edited by David Brady and Linda M. Burton, 48–74. Oxford: Oxford University Press, 2016.

Felitti, Vincent J., R. F. Anda, D. Nordenberg, D. F. Williamson, A. M. Spitz, V. Edwards, M. P. Koss, and J. S. Marks. "Relationship of Childhood Abuse and Household Dysfunction to Many of the Leading Causes of Death in Adults: The Adverse Childhood Experiences (ACE) Study." *American Journal of Preventive Medicine* 14, no. 4 (1998): 245–258.

Fernandez, Leondra. "Empathy and Social Justice: The Power of Proximity in Improvement Science." *Carnegie Commons* (blog), April 21, 2016. https://tinyurl.com/y3ypz24f.

Fowl, Stephen. *Idolatry*. Waco, TX: Baylor University Press, 2019.

Frazier, E. Franklin. *The Negro Church in America*. New York: Schocken, 1963.

Frederick, Marla. *Between Sundays: Black Women and Everyday Struggles of Faith*. Berkeley: University of California Press, 2003.

———. *Colored Television: American Religion Gone Global*. Stanford, CA: Stanford University Press, 2016.

Fulkerson, Mary McClintock. *Changing the Subject: Women's Discourses and Feminist Theology*. Minneapolis: Fortress, 1994.

———. *Places of Redemption: Theology for a Worldly Church*. New York: Oxford University Press, 2007.

Galtung, Johan. "Cultural Violence." *Journal of Peace Research* 27, no. 3 (1990): 295. https://www.jstor.org/stable/423472.

———. "Violence, Peace, and Peace Research." *Journal of Peace Research* 6, no. 3 (1969): 167–191. https://www.jstor.org/stable/422690.

Gibbons, Andrea. "The Five Refusals of White Supremacy." *American Journal of Economics and Sociology* 77, nos. 3–4 (May–September 2018): 729–755.

Gilbert, Kenyatta. *Exodus Preaching: Crafting Sermons about Justice and Hope*. Nashville: Abingdon, 2018.

Goizueta, Roberto. "Knowing the God of the Poor: The Preferential Option for the Poor." In *Opting for the Margins: Postmodernity and Liberation in Christian Theology*, edited by Joerg Rieger, 143–156. New York: Oxford University Press, 2003.

Goldstone, Brian. "The New American Homeless." *New Republic*, August 21, 2019. https://tinyurl.com/yy446hpc.

Graeber, David, and Thomas Piketty. "Soak the Rich." *Baffler*, July 2014. https://thebaffler.com/odds-and-ends/soak-the-rich.

Grant, Jacqueline. "The Sin of Servanthood and the Deliverance of Discipleship." In *A Troubling in My Soul: Womanist Perspectives on Evil and Suffering*, edited by Emilie Townes, 199–217. Maryknoll, NY: Orbis, 1993.

Griffith, R. Marie. *God's Daughters: Evangelical Women and the Power of Submission*. Berkeley: University of California Press, 1997.

Gutierrez, Gustavo. *A Theology of Liberation: History, Politics, and Salvation*. Rev. ed. Maryknoll, NY: Orbis, 2004.

Hall, David, ed. *Lived Religion in America: Toward a Theory of Practice*. Princeton, NJ: Princeton University Press, 1997.

Heath, Shirley Brice. "Protean Shapes in Literacy Events: Ever-Shifting Oral and Literate Traditions." In *Spoken and Written Language: Advances in Discourse Processes*, edited by Deborah Tannen, 91–118. Norwood, NJ: Ablex, 1982.

Hendersonville Times-News, April 30, 1985.

Himes, Kenneth, Lisa Sowle Cahill, Charles E. Curran, David Hollenbach, and Thomas A. Shannon, eds. *Modern Catholic Social Teaching.* Washington, DC: Georgetown University Press, 2005.

Holton, M. Jan. *Longing for Home: Forced Displacement and Postures of Hospitality.* New Haven, CT: Yale University Press, 2016.

Hoyt, Thomas, Jr. "Interpreting Biblical Scholarship for the Black Church Tradition." In *Stony the Road We Trod: African American Biblical Interpretation*, edited by Cain Hope Felder, 17–39. Minneapolis: Augsburg Fortress, 1991.

———. "Testimony." In *Practicing Our Faith: A Way of Life for a Searching People*, edited by Dorothy C. Bass, 89–102. San Francisco: Jossey-Bass, 2011.

Human Rights Council. "Report of the Special Rapporteur on Extreme Poverty and Human Rights on His Mission to the United States of America." Thirty-eighth session, June 18–July 6, 2018. http://undocs .org/A/HRC/38/33/ADD.1.

Jensen, George H. *Storytelling in Alcoholics Anonymous: A Rhetorical Analysis.* Carbondale: Southern Illinois University Press, 2000.

Johnson, Cedric. *Race, Religion, and Resilience in the Neoliberal Age.* New York: Palgrave MacMillan, 2016.

Jones, Beverly, Claudia Egelhoff, and Roger Manley. *Working in Tobacco: An Oral History of Durham's Tobacco Factory Workers.* Durham: History Department, North Carolina Central University, 1987.

Jones, Serene. *Feminist Theory and Christian Theology: Cartographies of Grace.* Minneapolis: Augsburg Fortress, 2000.

Jost, J., K. Hopper, T. Hay, S. Welber, and G. Haugland. "Homelessness, Severe Mental Illness, and the Institutional Circuit." *Psychiatric Services* 48, no. 5 (1997): 659–664.

Katz, Michael B. *The Undeserving Poor: America's Enduring Confrontation with Poverty.* Oxford: Oxford University Press, 2013.

Kling, David. *The Bible in History: How the Texts Have Shaped the Times.* New York: Oxford University Press, 2006.

LaMothe, Ryan. "Neoliberal Capitalism and the Corruption of Society: A Pastoral Political Analysis." *Pastoral Psychology* 65, no. 1 (2016): 5–21. https://doi.org/10.1007/s11089-013-0577-x.

———. *Pastoral Reflections on Global Citizenship: Framing the Political in Terms of Faith, Care, and Community.* London: Lexington, 2018.

Larner, Brad, and Adrian Blow. "A Model of Meaning-Making, Coping and Growth in Combat Veterans." *Review of General Psychology* 15, no. 3 (2011): 187–197.

LaRue, Cleophus. "The Exodus as Paradigmatic Text in the African American Community." In *Reclaiming the Imagination: The Exodus as Paradigmatic Narrative for Preaching*, edited by Dave Bland and David Fleer, 119–128. St. Louis: Chalice, 2009.

———. *I Believe I'll Testify: The Art of African American Preaching*. Louisville, KY: Westminster John Knox, 2011.

Lawson, Reneta. "Critical Race Theory as Praxis: A View from Outside to Outside." *Howard Law Journal* 38, no. 2 (1995): 353.

Lee, Barrett, Kimberly A. Tyler, and James D. Wright. "The New Homelessness Revisited." *Annual Review of Sociology* 36 (August 2010): 501–521.

Le Fevre, Mylon. "Without Him I Could Do Nothing." In *African American Heritage Hymnal*, edited by Rev. Dr. Delores Carpenter and Rev. Nolan E. Williams Jr., hymn 515. Chicago: GIA, 2001.

Lester, Andrew. *Hope in Pastoral Care and Counseling*. Louisville, KY: Westminster John Knox, 1995.

Levin, Josh. *The Queen: The Forgotten Life behind an American Myth*. New York: Little, Brown, 2019.

Lincoln, C. Eric. *Race, Religion, and the Continuing American Dilemma*. New York: Hill and Wang, 1984.

Lincoln, C. Eric, and Lawrence H. Mamiya. *The Black Church in the African American Experience*. Durham, NC: Duke University Press, 1990.

Love, Velma E. "Scriptures as Sundials in African American Lives." In *MisReading America: Scriptures and Difference*, edited by Vincent L. Wimbush, 86–116. New York: Oxford University Press, 2013.

Lowary, Wesley. "Paul Ryan, Poverty, Dog Whistles, and Electoral Politics." *Washington Post*, March 18, 2014. https://tinyurl.com/y56t9j7p.

Lowe, Walter. *Theology and Difference: The Wound of Reason*. Bloomington: Indiana University Press, 1993.

Mavelli, Luca. "Neoliberalism as Religion: Sacralization of the Market and Post-truth Politics." *International Political Sociology* 14, no. 1 (2020): 57–76.

Maynes, Mary Jo, Jennifer L. Pierce, and Barbara Laslett. *Telling Stories: The Use of Personal Narratives in the Social Sciences and History*. Ithaca, NY: Cornell University Press, 2008.

McClure, Barbara J. "The Social Construction of Emotions: A New Direction in the Pastoral Work of Healing." *Pastoral Psychology* 59, no. 6 (2010): 799–812.

McGuire, Meredith. *Lived Religion: Faith and Practice in Everyday Life*. New York: Oxford University Press, 2008.

Miller-McLemore, Bonnie. "The Contributions of Practical Theology." In *The Wiley-Blackwell Companion to Practical Theology*, edited by Bonnie Miller-McLemore, 1–20. Malden, MA: Wiley-Blackwell, 2012.

———. "Practical Theology." In *Encyclopedia of Religion in America*, edited by Charles H. Lippy and Peter Williams, 1739–1743. Washington, DC: CQ, 2010.

Mitchell, Henry H. *Black Preaching: The Recovery of a Powerful Art*. Nashville: Abingdon, 1990.

Mitchem, Stephanie. "Jesus Is My Doctor: Healing and Religion in African American Women's Lives." In *Religion and Healing in America*, edited by Linda L. Barnes, and Susan Starr Sered, 281–289. New York: Oxford University Press, 2005.

Morgan, David. *Religion and Material Culture: The Matter of Belief*. New York: Routledge, 2010.

Nelson, Timothy. *Every Time I Feel the Spirit: Religious Experience and Ritual in an African American Church*. New York: New York University Press, 2005.

Neuger, Christie Cozad. *Counseling Women: A Narrative, Pastoral Approach*. Minneapolis: Fortress, 2001.

Noe, Killian. *Finding Our Way Home: Addictions and Divine Love*. Scottsdale, PA: Herald, 2003.

Ong, Walter. *Orality and Literacy: The Technologizing of the Word*. New York: Routledge, 2002.

Orsi, Robert. "Is the Study of Lived Religion Irrelevant to the World We Live In?" *Journal of the Scientific Study of Religion* 42, no. 2 (2003): 169–174.

Park, C. L. "Trauma and Meaning Making: Converging Conceptualizations and Emerging Evidence." In *The Experience of Meaning in Life: Classical Perspectives, Emerging Themes, and Controversies*, edited by J. Hicks and C. Routledge, 61–76. Dordrecht, Netherlands: Springer, 2013.

Petrella, Ivan. *Beyond Liberation Theology: A Polemic*. London: SCM, 2008.

Pew Research Center. "Prayer in America." Accessed January 15, 2019. https://tinyurl.com/y3f3hs4u.

———. "Religious Landscape Study." Accessed January 15, 2019. https://tinyurl.com/yaontunx.

Pinn, Anthony. "Sweaty Bodies in a Circle: Thoughts on the Subtle Dimensions of Black Religion as Protest." *Black Theology: An International Journal* 4, no. 1 (2006): 11–26.

———. "Warm Bodies, Cold Currency: A Study of Religion's Response to Poverty." In *Religion and Poverty: Pan-African Perspectives*, edited by Peter J. Paris, 228–246. Durham, NC: Duke University Press, 2009.

Poole, W. Scott. *Satan in America: The Devil We Know*. Lanham, MD: Rowman & Littlefield, 2009.

Prahlad, Sw. Anand. *African-American Proverbs in Context*. Jackson: University of Mississippi, 1996.

Presbyterian Church (USA). "The Confession of Belhar." In *The Book of Confessions*, 300–306. Louisville, KY: Westminster John Knox, 2017.

Rankine, Claudia. "The Condition of Black Life Is One of Mourning." *New York Times*, June 22, 2015. https://tinyurl.com/y79ug5rd.

Reavis, James A., Jan Looman, Kristina A. Franco, and Briana Rojas. "Adverse Childhood Experiences and Adult Criminality: How Long Must We Live before We Possess Our Own Lives?" *Permanente Journal* 17, no. 2 (2013): 44–48.

Roberts, Chris. "The Great Eliminator: How Reagan Made Homelessness Permanent." *San Francisco Weekly*, June 29, 2016. https://tinyurl .com/y34fmjen.

Rogers-Vaughn, Bruce. *Care for Souls in a Neoliberal Age*. London: Palgrave Macmillan, 2016.

———. "Powers and Principalities: Initial Reflections toward a Post-capitalist Pastoral Theology." *Journal of Pastoral Theology* 25, no. 2 (December 2015): 71–92. https://doi.org/10.1179/1064986715Z .00000000010.

Rosenblatt, Paul C., and Beverly R. Wallace. *African American Grief*. New York: Routledge, 2005.

Rosmarin, David, Elizabeth J. Krumrei, and Kenneth I. Pargament. "Are Gratitude and Spirituality Protective Factors against Psychopathology?" *International Journal of Existential Psychology & Psychotherapy* 3, no. 1 (2010): 1–5.

Saar, Malika Saada, Yasmin Vafa, Rebecca Epstein, and Lindsay Rosenthal. "The Sexual Abuse to Prison Pipeline: The Girls' Story." Center for Poverty and Inequality. Georgetown University Law Center.

Sacks, Oliver. *Musicophilia: Tales of Music and the Brain*. New York: Knopf, 2007.

Sample, Tex. *Ministry in an Oral Culture: Living with Will Rogers, Uncle Remus, and Minnie Pearl*. Louisville, KY: Westminster John Knox, 1994.

Schache, Kiralee, Nathan Consedine, Paul Hofman, and Anna Serlachius. "Gratitude—More Than Just a Platitude? The Science behind Gratitude and Health." *British Journal of Health Psychology* 24, no. 1 (2018): 1–9.

Scharen, Christian, and Aana Marie Vigen, eds. *Ethnography as Christian Theology and Ethics*. New York: Continuum, 2011.

Scheib, Karen D. *Pastoral Care: Telling the Stories of Our Lives*. Nashville: Abingdon, 2016.

Scheper-Hughes, Nancy. *Death without Weeping: The Violence of Everyday Life in Brazil*. Berkeley: University of California Press, 1992.

Sears, Edmund H. "It Came upon the Midnight Clear." In *Glory to God: The Presbyterian Hymnal*, edited by David Eicher, hymn 123. Louisville, KY: Westminster John Knox, 2013.

Semega, Jessica L., Kayla R. Fontenot, and Melissa A. Kollar. "Income and Poverty in the United States: 2016—Current Population Reports." US Census Bureau, September 2017. https://tinyurl.com/y7lat5gn.

Sharp, Melinda A. McGarrah. *Misunderstanding Stories: Toward a Postcolonial Pastoral Theology*. Eugene, OR: Pickwick, 2013.

Shelton, Jason E., and Michael O. Emerson. *Blacks and Whites in Christian America: How Racial Discrimination Shapes Religious Convictions.* New York: New York University Press, 2012.

Shepherd, Phillis Isabella. "Womanist Pastoral Theology and Black Women's Experience of Gender, Religion, and Sexuality." In *Pastoral Theology and Care: Critical Trajectories in Theory and Practice,* edited by Nancy J. Ramsay, 125–147. Hoboken, NJ: John Wiley & Sons, 2018.

Sims, Angela D. *Lynched: The Power of Memory in a Culture of Terror.* Waco, TX: Baylor University Press, 2016.

Smitherman, Geneva. *Talkin and Testifyin: The Language of Black America.* Boston: Houghton Mifflin, 1977.

Snodgrass, Jill. "Shelters or Sanctuaries: Practical Theology, Pastoral Care and Counseling, and Homelessness." PhD diss., Claremont School of Theology, 2010.

Solórzano, Daniel G., and Tara J. Yosso. "A Critical Race Counterstory of Race, Racism, and Affirmative Action." *Equity & Excellence in Education* 35, no. 2 (2002): 155–168.

Sorg, Lisa. "Take 5: Durham's Gentrification Challenge." *News and Observer,* November 3, 2015. https://tinyurl.com/y2vf62vd.

Soss, Joe, Richard C. Fording, and Sanford Schram. *Disciplining the Poor: Neoliberal Paternalism and the Persistent Power of Race.* Chicago: University of Chicago Press, 2011.

Spencer, Jon Michael. *Protest and Praise: Sacred Music of Black Religion.* Nashville: Fortress, 1990.

Stendl-Rast, David. *Gratefulness: The Heart of Prayer.* Ramsey, NJ: Paulist, 1984.

Stevenson, Bryan. Commencement speech at Johns Hopkins University, May 24, 2018. Available at https://tinyurl.com/y23789of.

Stivers, Laura. *Disrupting Homelessness: Alternative Christian Approaches.* Minneapolis: Fortress, 2011.

Stoltzfus, Regina Shands. "Couldn't Keep It to Myself: Testimony in the Black Church Tradition." *Vision: A Journal for Church and Theology* 10, no. 2 (2009): 43–49.

Sullivan, Susan Crawford. *Living Faith: Everyday Religion and Mothers in Poverty.* Chicago: University of Chicago Press, 2011.

Swidler, Ann. *Talk of Love: How Culture Matters.* Chicago: University of Chicago Press, 2001.

Tanner, Kathryn. *Theories of Culture: A New Agenda for Theology.* Minneapolis: Augsburg Fortress, 1997.

Taylor, Mark Lewis. "Subalternity and Advocacy as Kairos for Theology." In *Opting for the Margins: Postmodernity and Liberation in Christian Theology,* edited by Joerg Rieger, 23–44. New York: Oxford University Press, 2003.

Turner, Victor. *The Ritual Process: Structure and Anti-structure*. New York: Aldine de Gruyter, 1995.

Wacker, Grant. *Heaven Below: Early Pentecostals and American Culture*. Cambridge, MA: Harvard University Press, 2003.

Wacquant, Loïc. "The Penalisation of Poverty and the Rise of Neoliberalism." *European Journal on Criminal Policy and Research* 9, no. 4 (2001): 401–412. https://doi.org/10.1023/A:1013147404519.

———. "Scrutinizing the Street: Poverty, Morality, and the Pitfalls of Urban Ethnography." *American Journal of Sociology* 107, no. 6 (May 2002): 1468–1532.

Walker, Alice. *The Color Purple*. New York: Houghton Mifflin, 1982.

Warner, R. Stephen. Introduction to *Gatherings in Diaspora: Religious Communities and the New Migration*, edited by R. Stephen Warner and Judith G. Wittner. Philadelphia: Temple University Press, 1998.

Watkins, Philip C., Michael Van Gelder, and Araceli Frias. "Furthering the Science of Gratitude." In *The Oxford Handbook of Positive Psychology*, edited by Shane J. Lopez and C. R. Snyder, 437–446. 2nd ed. New York: Oxford University Press, 2009.

Watkins Ali, Carroll. *Survival and Liberation in African American Context*. St. Louis: Chalice, 1999.

Weiner, Eric. "Slum Visits: Tourism or Voyeurism?" *New York Times*, March 9, 2008. https://tinyurl.com/y3eb4ty6.

West, Traci. *Wounds of the Spirit: Black Women, Violence, and Resistance Ethics*. New York: New York University Press, 1999.

Wigg-Stevenson, Natalie. *Ethnographic Theology: An Inquiry into the Production of Theological Knowledge*. New York: Palgrave Macmillan, 2014.

Williams, Delores. *Sisters in the Wilderness: The Challenge of Womanist God-Talk*. Maryknoll, NY: Orbis, 1993.

Williams, Ingrid. "Durham Dining: Pies, Panini and Barbecue." *New York Times*, June 24, 2011. https://tinyurl.com/yy7wwcmq.

Wilmore, Gayraud. *Black Religion and Black Radicalism: An Interpretation of the Religious History of African Americans*. Maryknoll, NY: Orbis, 1998.

———. "Black Religion: Strategies of Survival, Elevation, and Liberation." *Journal of the Interdenominational Theological Center* 21, nos. 1–2 (Fall–Spring 1993–1994): 145–164.

Wilson, Jennie. "Hold to God's Unchanging Hand." In *African American Heritage Hymnal*, edited by Rev. Dr. Delores Carpenter and Rev. Nolan E. Williams Jr., hymn 404. Chicago: GIA, 2001.

Winfrey, Oprah. "6 Things We Know for Sure about the Power of Gratitude." Oprah.com. Accessed January 11, 2019. https://tinyurl.com/y5ecqlca.

Wink, Walter. *The Powers That Be: Theology for a New Millennium.* New York: Doubleday, 1998.

Wolgemuth, Jennifer R. "Analyzing for Critical Resistance in Narrative Research." *Qualitative Research* 14, no. 5 (2014): 586–602.

World Communion of Reformed Churches. "The Accra Confession." 2004. https://wcrc.ch/accra/the-accra-confession.

Yancy, George, and Judith Butler. "What's Wrong with All Lives Matter?" *New York Times*, January 12, 2015. https://tinyurl.com/yyctbd7r.

Yosso, Tara J. "Whose Culture Has Capital? A Critical Race Theory Discussion of Community Cultural Wealth." *Race Ethnicity and Education* 8, no. 1 (2005): 69–91.

INDEX